a beginner's guide to origami

a beginner's guide to origami

easy step-by-step projects

Nick Robinson

p

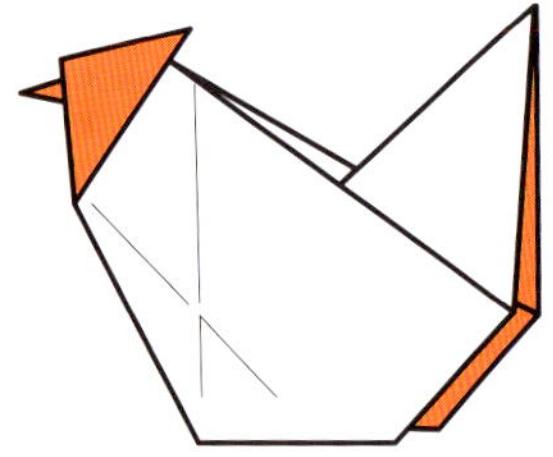

This is a Parragon Publishing book
First published in 2005

Parragon Publishing
Queen Street House
4 Queen Street
Bath, BA1 1HE, UK

Design by Design Principals, Warminster

Text and diagrams by Nick Robinson

ISBN 1-40546-061-X
Printed in China

Contents

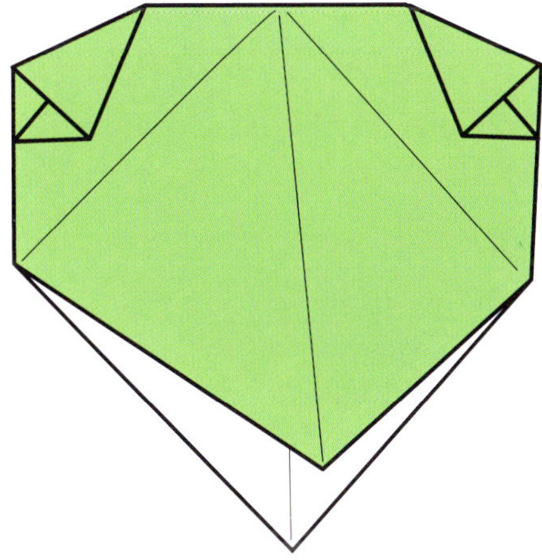

Introduction

Origami is a Japanese word made from two shorter words, "Ori" meaning to fold and "Kami" meaning paper. Thus "origami" refers to the art of paper-folding. Traditionally, it consisted of a series of simple, stylized designs, but during the last 50 years, it has blossomed to an extraordinary extent.

History

Origami has its origins in China around the first century C.E., when paper as we know it was believed to have been invented. By the sixth century, it had spread to Japan, where it was a rare commodity, to be treasured. The Japanese incorporated paper into their worship and a few designs still survive from these times. As time and technology moved on, paper was increasingly available and affordable, and origami began to permeate the whole of Japanese society, from the very young to the very old.

The oldest published set of origami instructions is called the "Senbazuru Orikata," or "How to Fold One Thousand Cranes." This dates back to 1797 and shows a method for cutting a large sheet of paper in such a way that 100 cranes, all joined together, can be folded from it. The first real collection of origami diagrams (1845) was called the "Kan no modo" ("Window on Midwinter"). It included many subjects, including dragonflies and crabs.

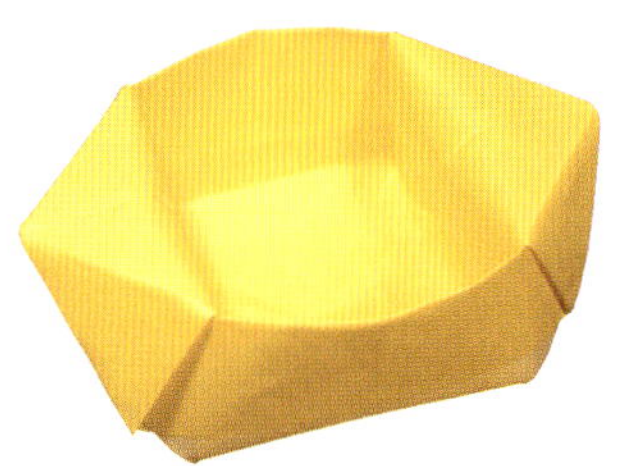

It is believed that Muslims from Africa may have brought paper-folding with them when they invaded Spain in the eighth century. A tradition was established in Spain that survives to this day. Among its foremost proponents was the philosopher Miguel de Unamuno (1864-1936).

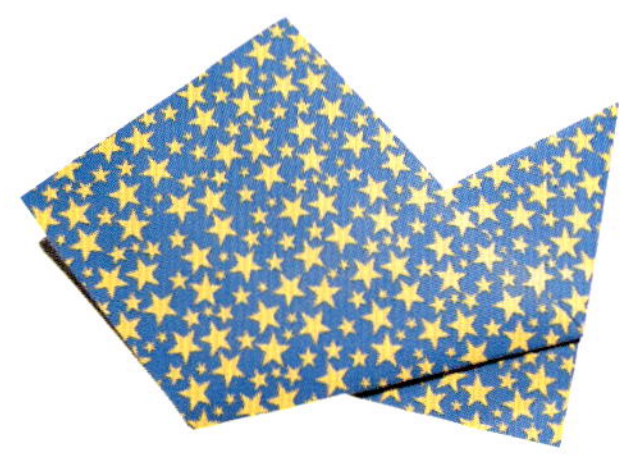

In Bad Blankenburg in Germany, Friedrich Froebel (1782-1852) established his (then) revolutionary ideas about education and the kindergarten (literally "Garden of Children"). These ideas included the inclusion of paper-folding amongst several other geometric activities. Origami began to enter the British consciousness around the turn of the century, where the escapologist Houdini incorporated simple designs into his act. The "Boys' Own Paper," a contemporary comic book, included instructions for the classic "Flapping Bird."

Margaret Campbell wrote "Paper Toy Making" in 1936. This was the first book to present the idea of "Foundation Folds," now known as "bases." These were common opening sequences of folds used to create well-known models, such as the "bird base" and "fish base." Nowadays, we don't rely so heavily on bases, but at the time, it was a revolutionary discovery.

In the 1950s, a few enthusiasts, led by the magician Robert Harbin and the American Lillian Oppenheimer, began to forge contacts with other paper-folders, most notably Japanese master Akira Yoshizawa, now acknowledged as perhaps the foremost origami creator of our time.

An origami meeting in progress

The longest origami train in the world at York Railway Museum in England.

American folders, including Fred Rohm and Samual Randlett, began to develop new techniques and bases, and ground rules were established for the symbols used in origami diagrams.

This use of common symbols meant that the spoken or written language wasn't so important and has allowed origami to spread around the world. This has been continued and greatly expanded by the Internet. Nowadays, you can use the web to find huge amounts of information on all aspects of origami. There are many origami societies around the world, many of which have their own websites.

Paper

There are no rules about which types of paper can be used for origami—the simple answer is to try everything you can find. You'll soon discover how to identify paper that can be creased and will "remember" that crease. Some types of cheap colored paper too brittle to be of much use. Other paper may be too thick for folding complex designs. For your first attempts, don't worry about the paper too much—the first task is to understand and follow the diagrams, so your fingers can get used to the various moves required. Later, when you have mastered the folding sequence, you can start to think about what paper will best suit the finished model.

Creator Paul Hanson has a black belt in origami.

Remember to consider both color and texture. Conventional origami paper is colored on one side, white on the other. It is (or should be) perfectly square. This is perfect for practicing or for teaching—the paper is easy to crease and usually of a bright color. However, it rarely has much by way of texture. You should branch out and consider brown kraft paper, Ingres, or other types of art paper, wallpaper, anything you can find. There are specialist origami papers called chiyogami and washi, each with their own special qualities. Some folders even create their own paper by using spray glue to attach a sheet of foil to a sheet of tissue paper. This gives a wonderful iridescent quality, perfect for making insects. However, foil paper is notably difficult when you want to unfold a crease and fold it back on itself.

Paper doesn't always come in the proper sized squares you need. The answer is to buy large sheets, then trim them down to the correct size. You can use a sharp knife with a steel ruler and cutting-board, but there is always the danger of accidents. If you're serious, you should buy a rotary paper cutter—the smaller models are very reasonably priced. You'll then need a set of narrow drawers or filing trays in which to keep your paper. You should store it inside plastic envelopes, since paper can absorb moisture from the air and it will then become almost useless for correct folding.

Folding techniques

Anyone can make ugly origami—just fold quickly and carelessly! There is no magic to making beautiful origami, it just needs time, patience, and a willingness to practice. When folding a model for the first time, you need to work out what the diagrams are telling you. This may not be obvious and you'll probably put in many creases you don't need. The paper becomes tired and worn. This is not a bad thing—each time you make it, the result will be neater. Finally, after anything from 3 through 30 repetitions of a design, you'll know it well enough to concentrate on the fine details—sharp points, no "white bits" sticking out, and so on. Many people assume their first effort will be enough, but you may not even finish a design on your first visit. It will all depend on how well you understand the symbols, whether you've bothered to read the text instructions as well, whether you have worked in sequence through the book or dived straight in with a complex design.

Symbols

Origami diagrams use a set of symbols created by Akira Yoshizawa and refined by Sam Randlett. Their usage may vary slightly, but once you recognize them, you'll be able to follow a diagram even if the language isn't familiar to you. There is a basic set of symbols common to all, then a few extra ones that some people like to use. The whole purpose of them is to make clear what it is you need to do with the paper.

Turn paper around

Diagram is enlarged

Turn paper over

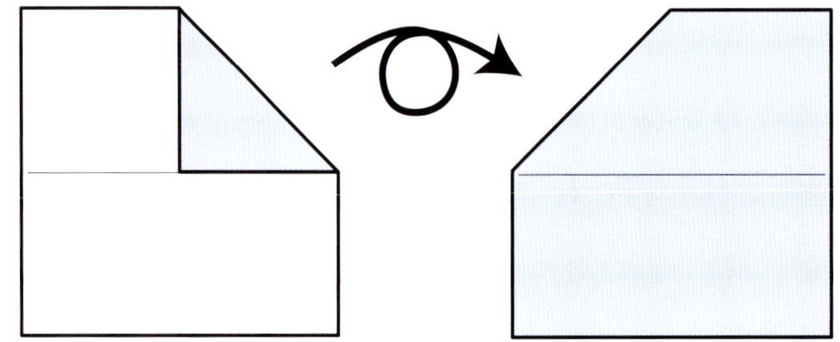

Squash fold

With a squash fold, part of the paper is flattened in the direction of the arrow. Here is the way it's shown.

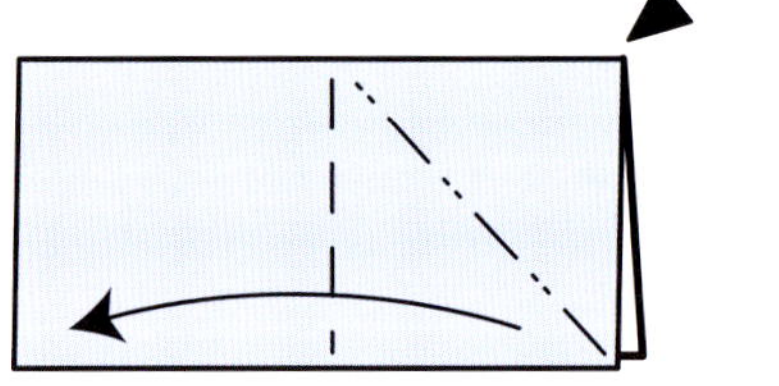

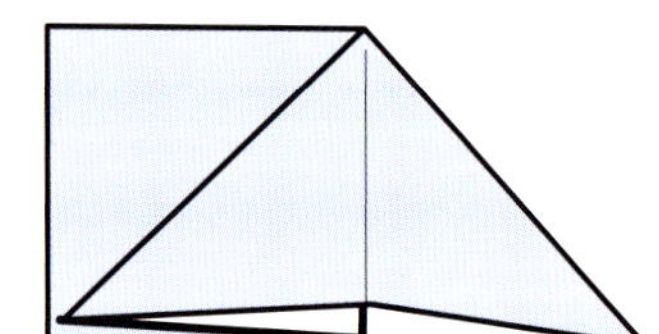

Valley crease (dashed line)

This is the most widely-used crease, for example when folding a sheet of paper in half. Always line up the edges and shuffle them backward and forward until the paper is in the right position, then use one hand to hold the layers in place as you slide your finger down the center of the paper toward you. When it reaches the end, move your finger to one side then the other, forming the crease. Afterward, you can use both first fingers to reinforce the crease.

Valley fold

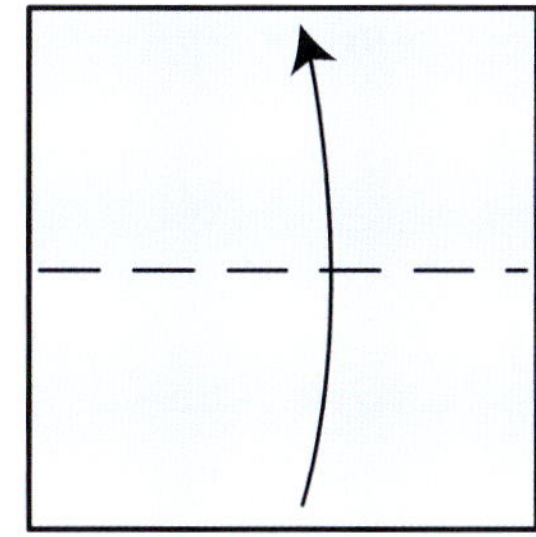

Valley and unfold

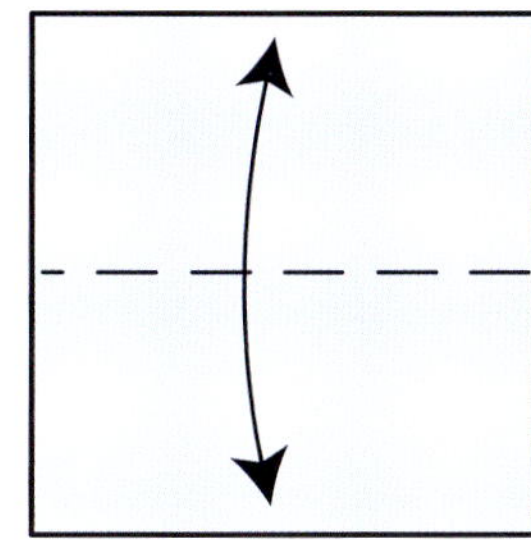

Mountain crease (dash with two dots)

This is the opposite to a valley crease, where part of the paper folds underneath. It's generally easiest to turn the paper upside down and make this as a valley fold, then turn the paper back over, so it matches the diagrams.

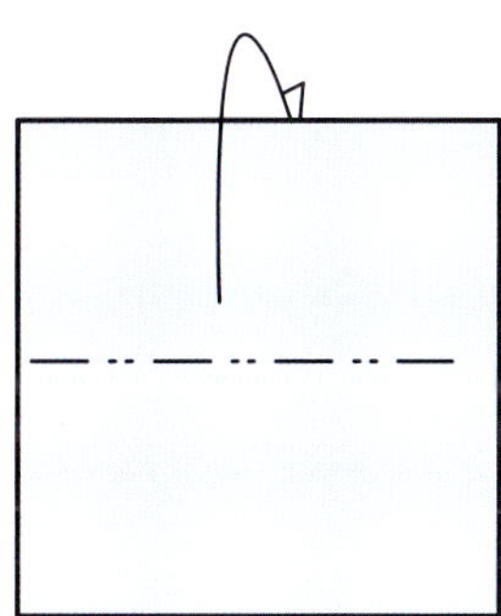

Repeat arrow

A dash through the arrow means the same fold or step is needed again. The number off dashes shows the number of repeats. This fold was repeated once on the opposite corner.

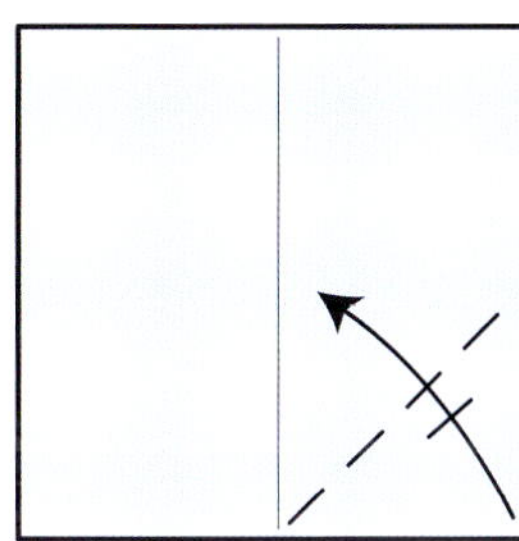

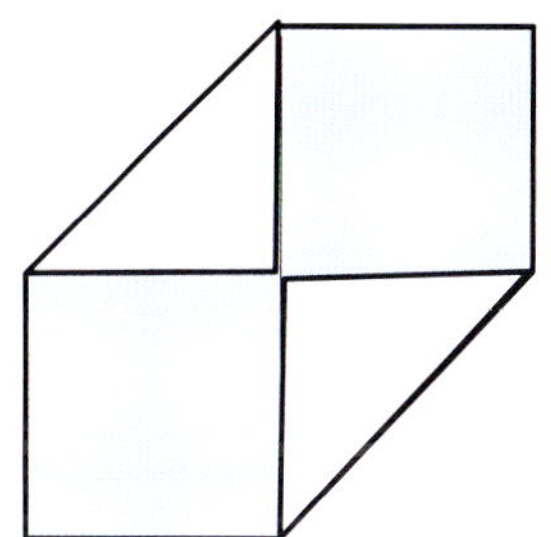

Techniques and Bases

When you look at the extraordinary things you can do with origami, it's easy to feel overwhelmed and to think "I could never do that!" But like all great creations, from music concertos to 3D computer games, they can be broken down into smaller techniques that can be worked on and adapted. While it's true that you can follow origami instructions in a mechanical, step-by-step approach, a fuller understanding of what is happening will allow you to get the most enjoyment from your folding. You will begin to appreciate that even the most complex designs make use of folds and moves that you learned on simple, schoolyard designs.

There's another good reason why you should try to develop a good grounding in origami technique—so you can start creating your own designs! Truly original origami designs are very rare—most start with either a traditional base, or adapt an existing design. In order to do this, you need to know the possibilities open to you at any given stage in the model. If you're making a bird, you'll need to know how to produce a beak. Elephants need large ears and a trunk. Every time you create, you'll draw upon the many possibilities within the paper in order to develop the model.

With all this in mind, you are strongly recommended to work through this initial section on techniques and bases. Play with the paper—keep folding and unfolding the paper until you fully understand the mechanics of the move. Keep your mind open to alternatives—see if you can turn a fold "inside out," try to alter angles and proportions. Each of the bases shown here can be folded in several different ways—unfold a completed base and see if you can discover a different folding method. Set yourself high standards—if you haven't made the creases perfectly, fold again and again until they are perfect. If you can't make these relatively simple folds properly, you will struggle with more complicated designs. Above all, enjoy yourself!

Hidden cross

Here's a simple challenge for you to practice, and check how the accuracy of your folds! Make two examples of this model, then see if you can arrange them to form the shape of a white cross. You can make a beautiful repeating pattern by arranging lots of similar models.

1 Fold in half from corner to opposite corner, crease and unfold. Do this both ways.

2 Now fold from side to opposite side and add the remaining diagonal creases.

3 Make a crease which passes through the center of the paper, so that the center of the lower edge lies on the upper-left diagonal. Check the next drawing for guidance and note how the creases line up at the circled areas. Don't make the crease until you're sure it's lined up properly!

4 This is the result. Fold down a triangular flap to line up with the edge underneath.

5 Repeat with the lower left corner.

6 The completed fold. Make two and form a cross.

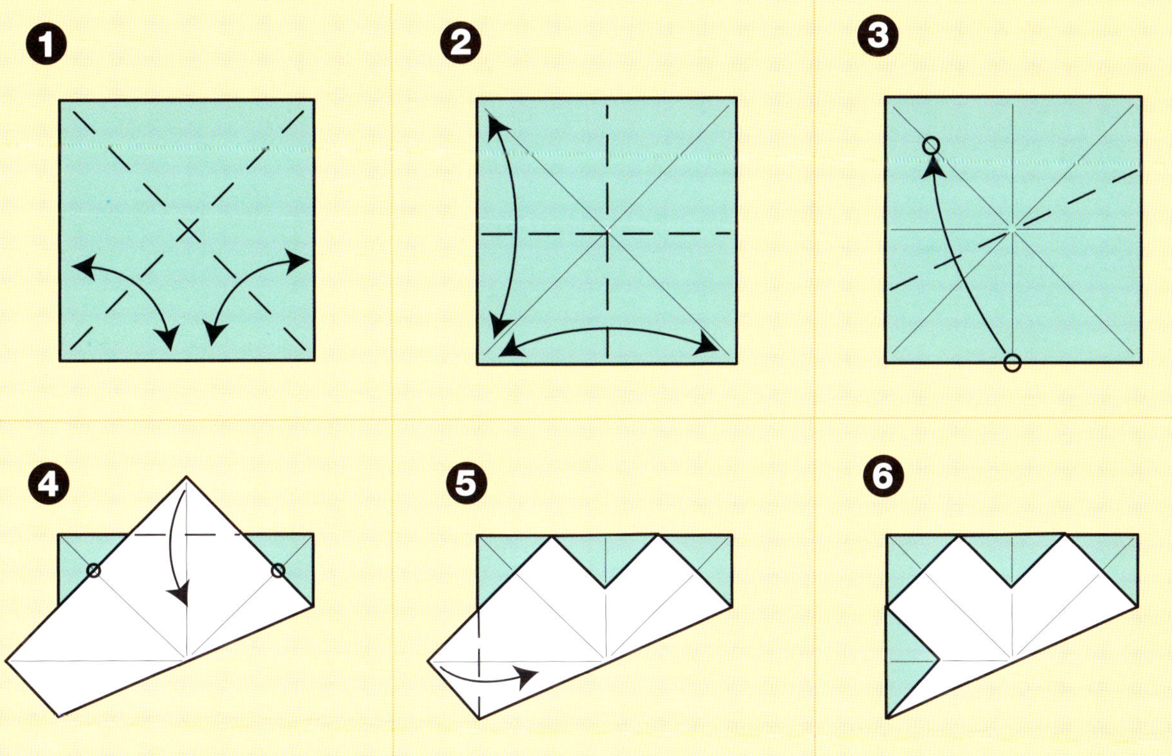

Outside reverse fold

These are vital to most origami models, so you should study them carefully and experiment to find all the different ways in which they can be used.

1 Start with a pointed flap, fold over at whatever angle you wish.

2 Crease firmly and unfold.

3 Open the paper out and fold one layer to each side, turning the paper inside out and reversing the direction of some of the creases.

4 The completed outside reverse fold.

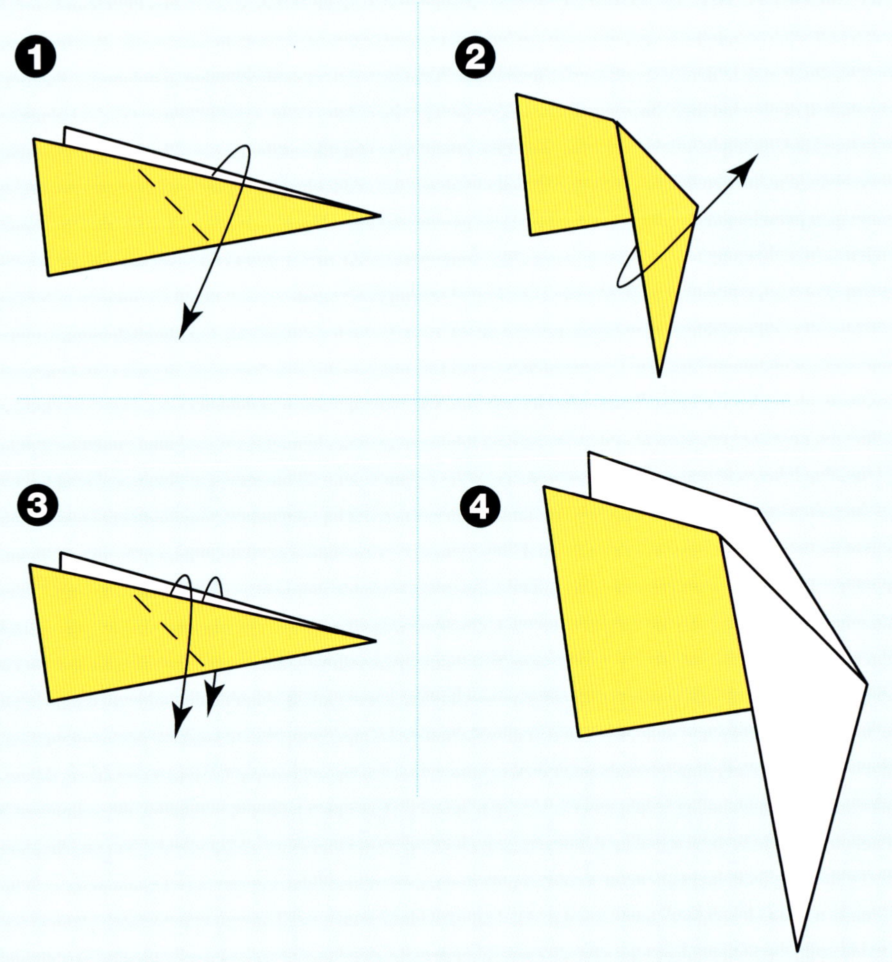

Inside reverse fold

Here, part of the paper folds inside the rest. Compare it to the outside reverse fold. A combination of the two is used to form beaks on a bird, for example.

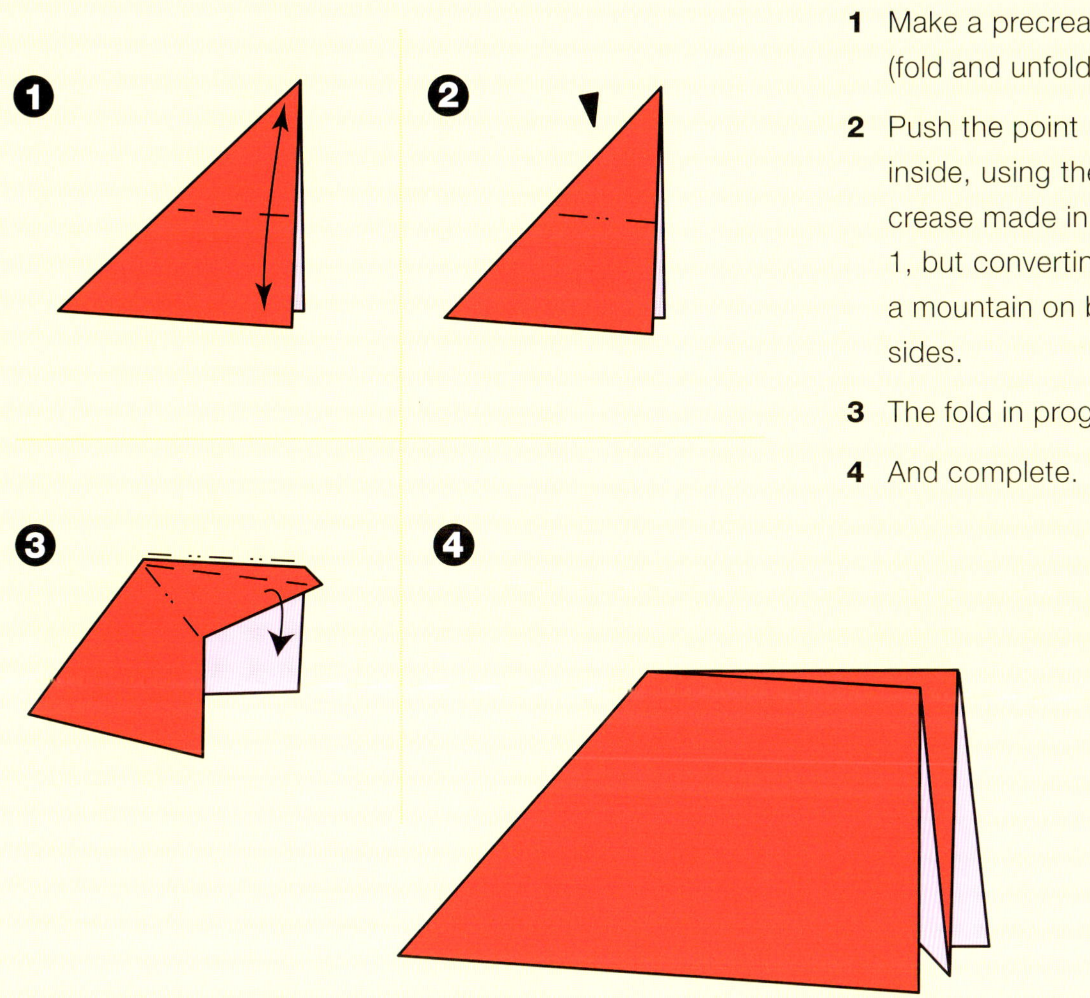

1 Make a precrease (fold and unfold).

2 Push the point inside, using the crease made in step 1, but converting it to a mountain on both sides.

3 The fold in progress.

4 And complete.

Rabbit's ear

This is used to form a colored point from a white corner and is used to create arms, ears, and many other parts of a model. Here it is folded on a square that has both diagonal creases.

1 Fold an edge to a diagonal, creasing only as far as the vertical diagonal.

2 Repeat the fold from the other side.

3 Fold in both sides together, adding a vertical valley crease at the center.

4 A central point is formed. Flatten this to one side or the other.

5 The completed rabbit's ear.

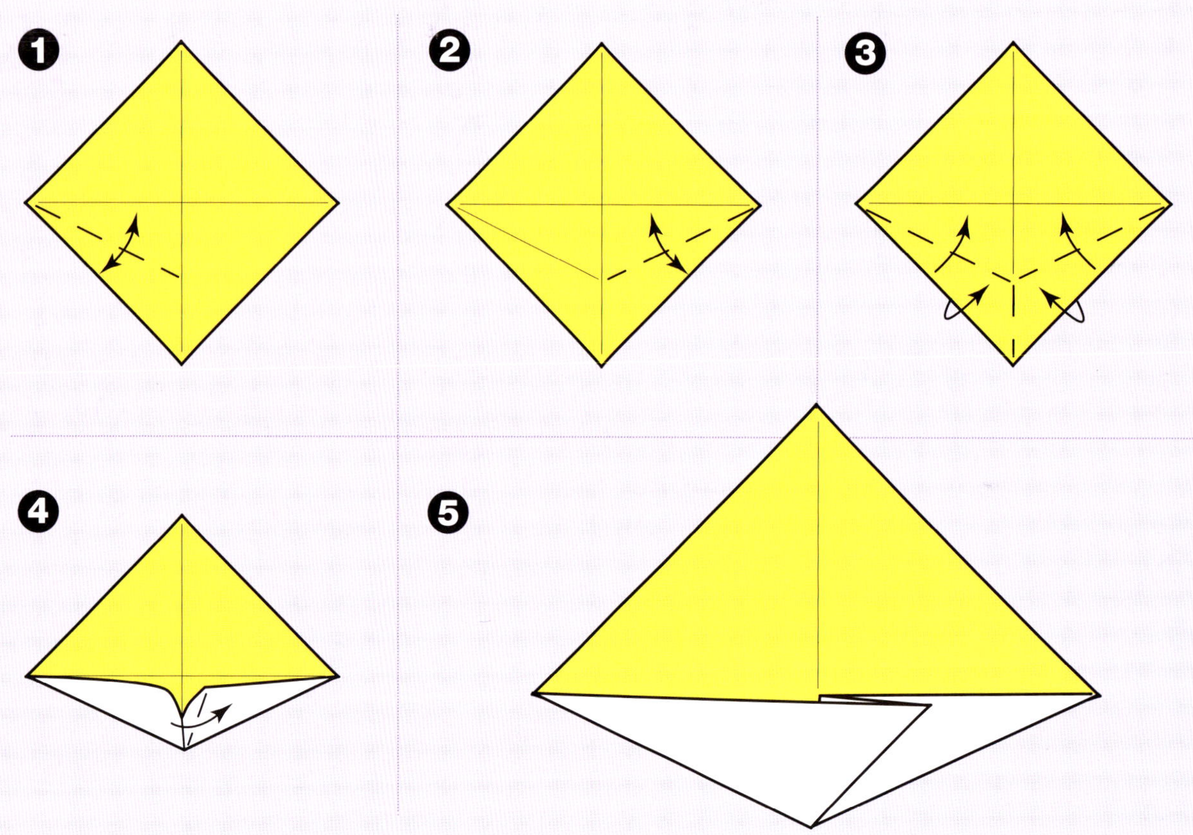

Kite base

Although simple, this base can be used as the starting point for make many different designs.

1 Fold a diagonal crease and unfold.

2 Fold the lower-right edge to the crease.

3 Repeat on the left-hand side.

4 The completed kite base.

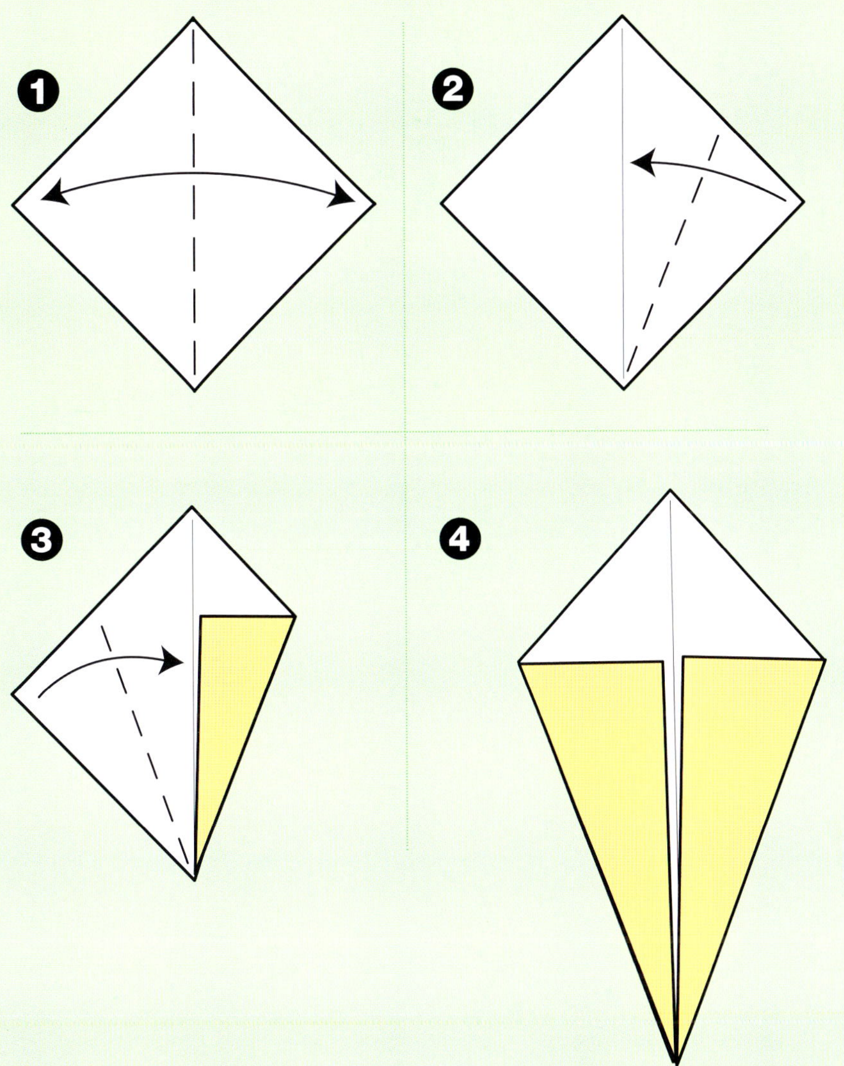

Preliminary base

This uses a crease pattern, in which the diagonals and the “side-to-side” creases are kitty corner (ie. two are valley, two are mountain folds).

1 Start with the colored side upward and crease both diagonals.

2 Turn the paper over and fold side-to-side both ways.

3 Use the creases shown to collapse the paper toward you.

4 The completed preliminary base.

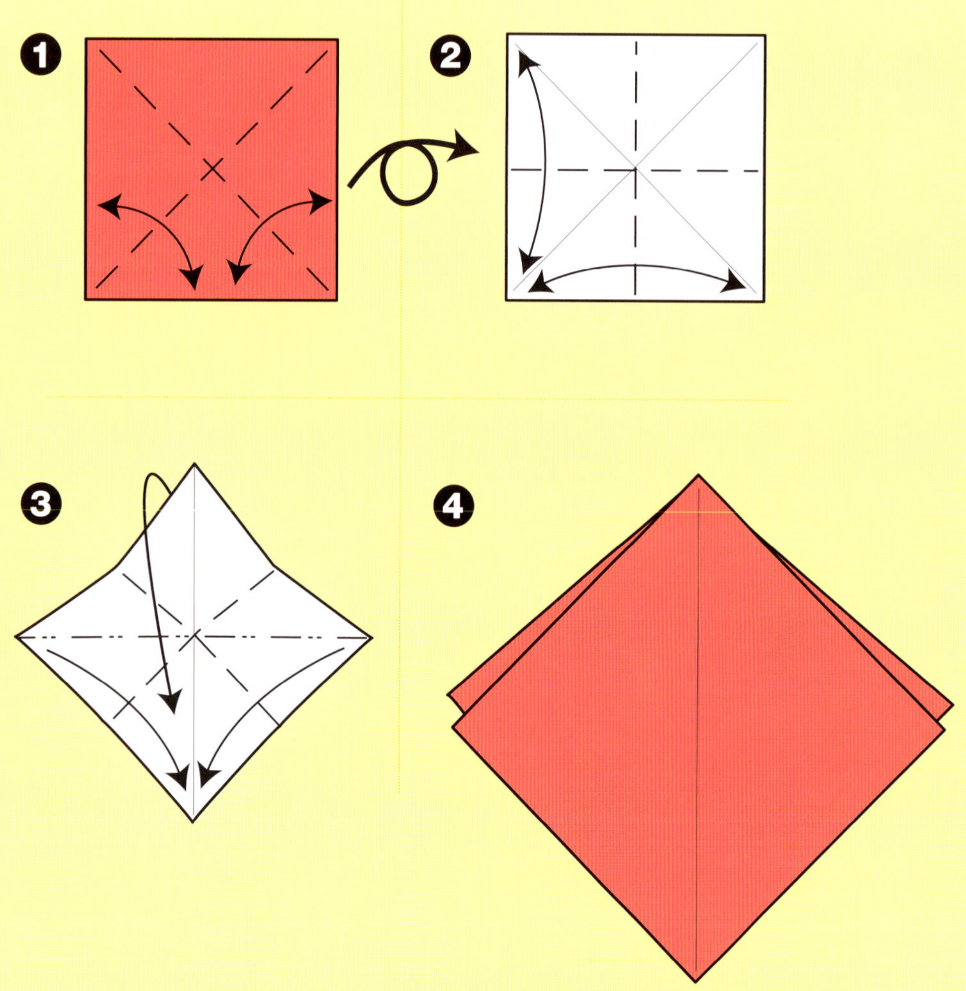

Waterbomb base

This uses an identical crease pattern to the preliminary base, but it folds the opposite way. You can, in fact, turn each one inside out to form the other.

1 Start with the colored side upward and fold side-to-side both ways.

2 Turn the paper over and crease both diagonals.

3 Use the creases shown to collapse the paper toward you.

4 The completed waterbomb base.

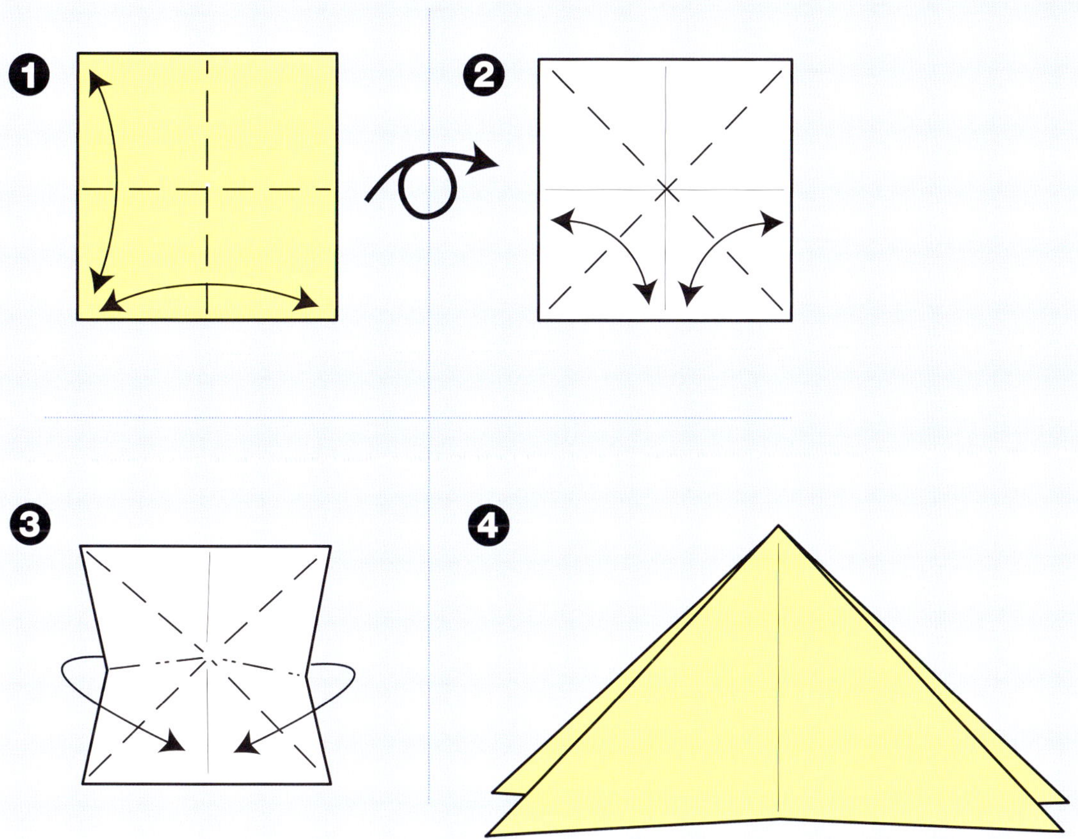

Blinz base

This is where all four corners are folded in to meet at the center. It is used in the traditional "fortune teller" that many people folded as a child. You can, of course, simply fold the corners in, but this isn't easy to do accurately. Instead, we can use the following procedure.

1 Fold the paper in half.

2 Fold each short edge to the top edge. Repeat the steps on the other side.

3 Unfold the lower triangular layer.

4 The completed blinz.

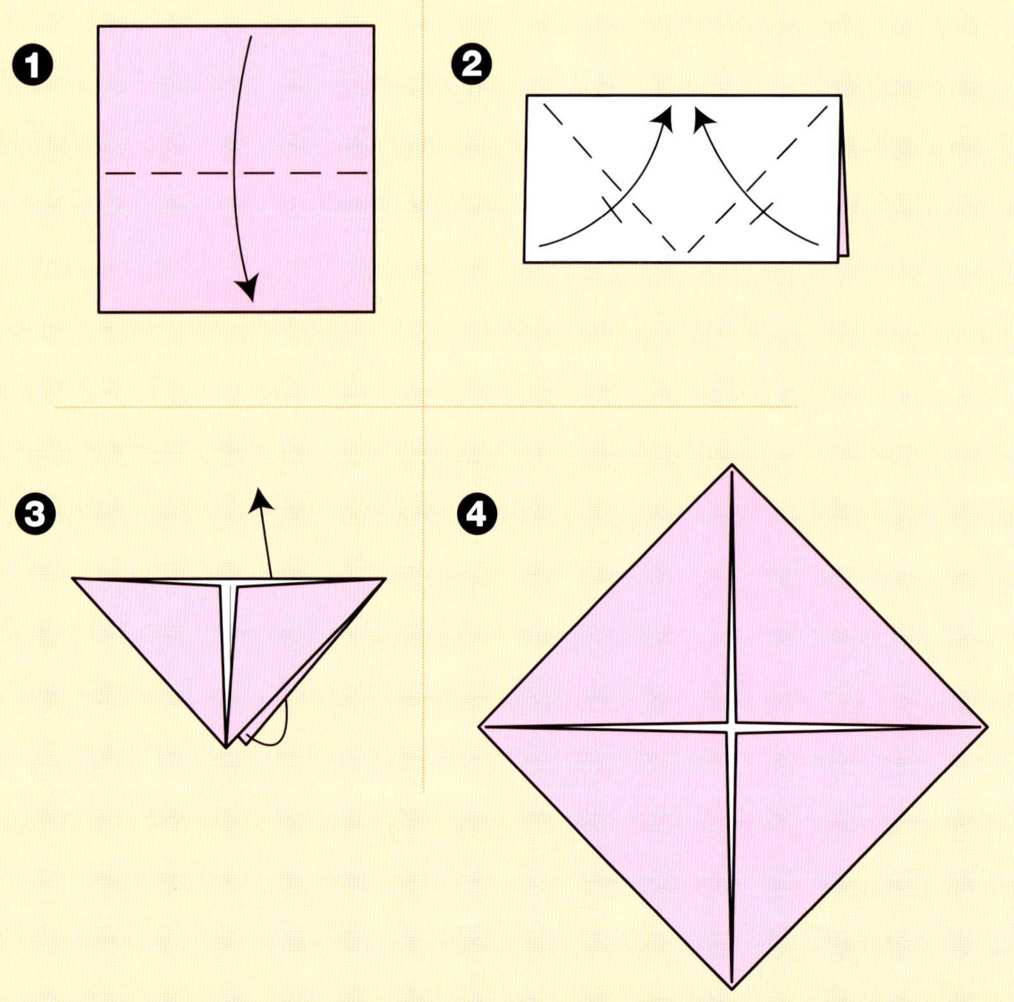

Fish base

Anther simple but versatile base, which actually consists of two rabbit ears, if you look closely.

1 Fold both diagonals.

2 Fold two edges to the crease, to make a kite base.

3 This is the result.

4 Turn the paper over and fold in half.

5 Put your fingers into the pockets and open them out, carefully flattening into points.

6 The fish base.

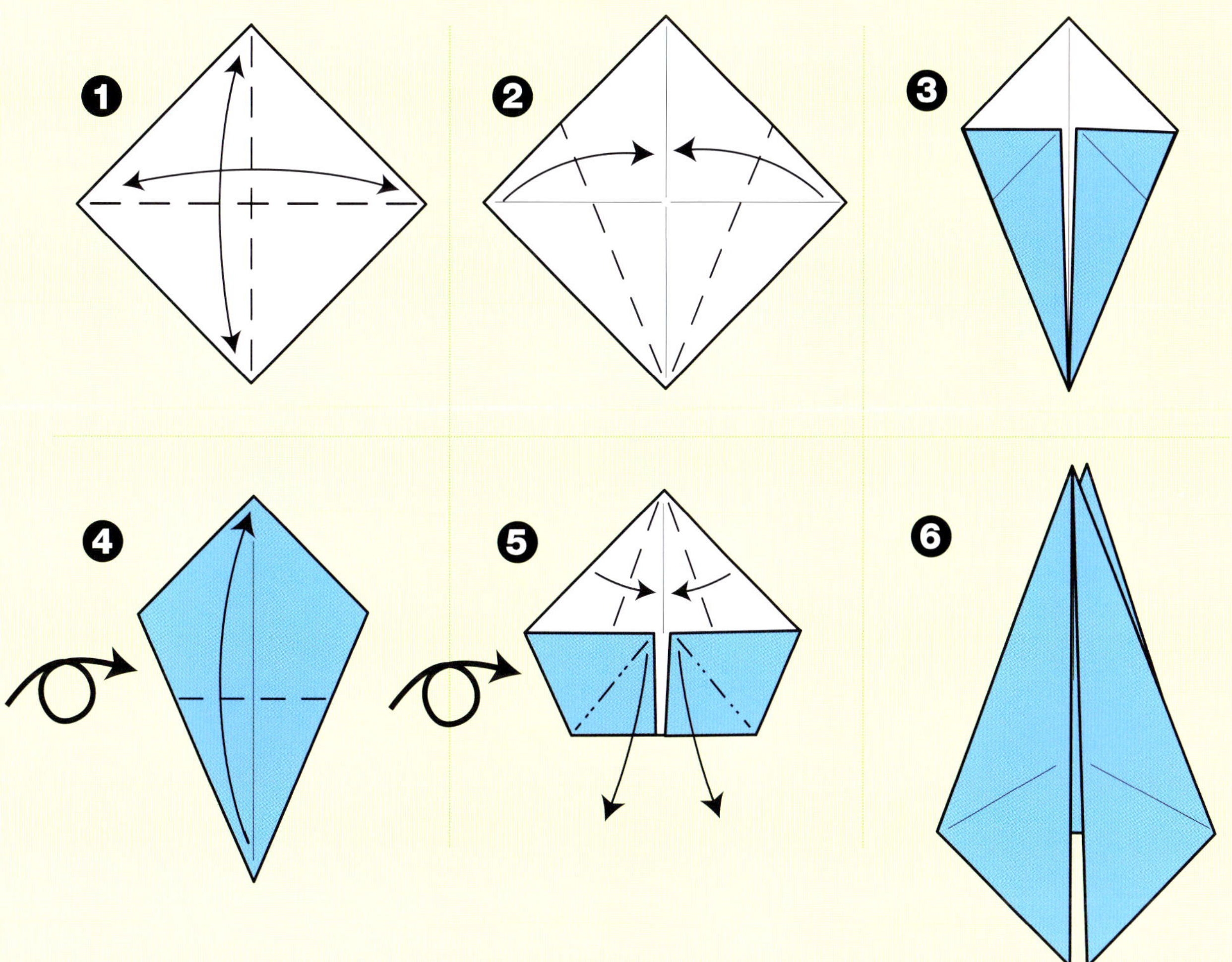

The Models

OK, now you've worked through the techniques and bases, you should have a good idea of what the symbols mean and you'll know how important it is to read the instructions carefully before completing each step, as well as the importance of careful, accurate folding. Remember to always look at the next diagram, so you know what you're aiming for! As you might expect, the designs have been placed in a suitable order for a beginner to fold. Unless you are an experienced folder, it's probably not a good idea to start with one of the later designs in the book, although there is nothing that would qualify as "complex" in origami terms.

You should first make the model a couple of times, using inexpensive paper. This will allow you to work out what the diagrams mean and let your fingers familiarize themselves with the moves. Fold the paper as many times as it takes for you to feel confident about making the model. Then take a sheet of your best paper and really concentrate on folding a perfect example. Take a few extra seconds over every crease, to make sure the paper is exactly where it should be before you make the crease.

Cat's head

One of the beauties of origami is the way in which it captures the essence of a subject with a few simple creases (in this case, seven). This design (a variation of a traditional design) also allows the folder to experiment by changing angles and distances to create other animals, or to make it look like your own idea of what a cat looks like. Start with a square, colored side down.

1. Fold the lower corner to the opposite corner.
2. Fold the two lower corners to meet the top corner.
3. Form the ears by folding the points down at an angle. Work out where to fold them by looking at the next diagram, although it isn't critical.
4. Fold up the small triangular flap.
5. Turn the paper over. Fold over the corner to make a nose.
6. Complete.

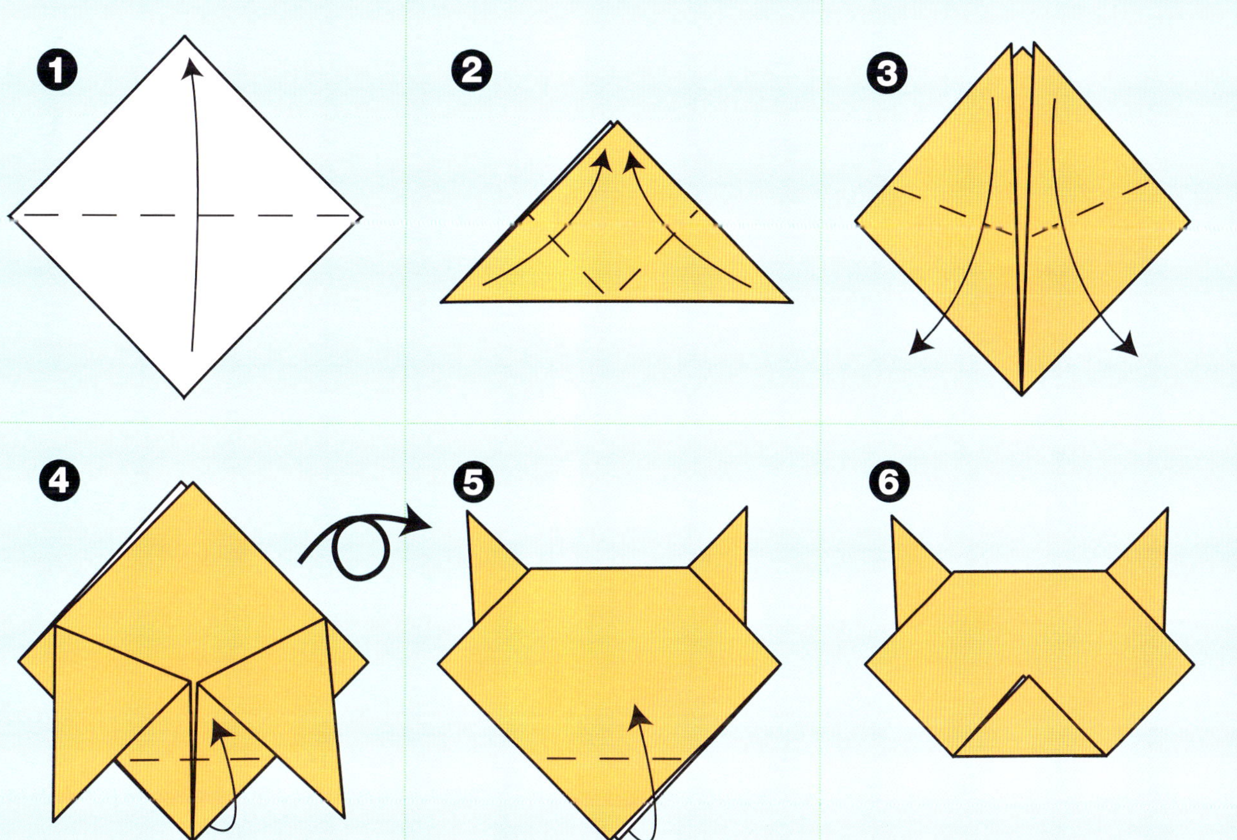

Bat

For many, the essence of origami is simplicity—capturing the subject with as few creases as possible. This design by the author is an example. Although it has no legs, it's still perfectly bat-like. If you can find it, choose a sheet of dark brown paper with a texture. You can add further creases to shape the wings if you like.

1 Start with a square, colored side down. Fold from corner to opposite corner.

2 Fold in half from side to side, crease firmly and unfold.

3 Fold the lower end of the crease to just short of the top (check the next drawing).

4 Fold the point down, leaving a small gap.

5 Fold in half behind on the existing crease.

6 Fold the wings up. The crease starts at the back of the head and extends to the bottom-right corner.

7 Fold the lower-right edge to the lower-left edge. Repeat underneath.

8 Fold both wingtips down—the crease goes from corner to corner.

9 Unfold the wings but leave them at a slight angle.

Complete.

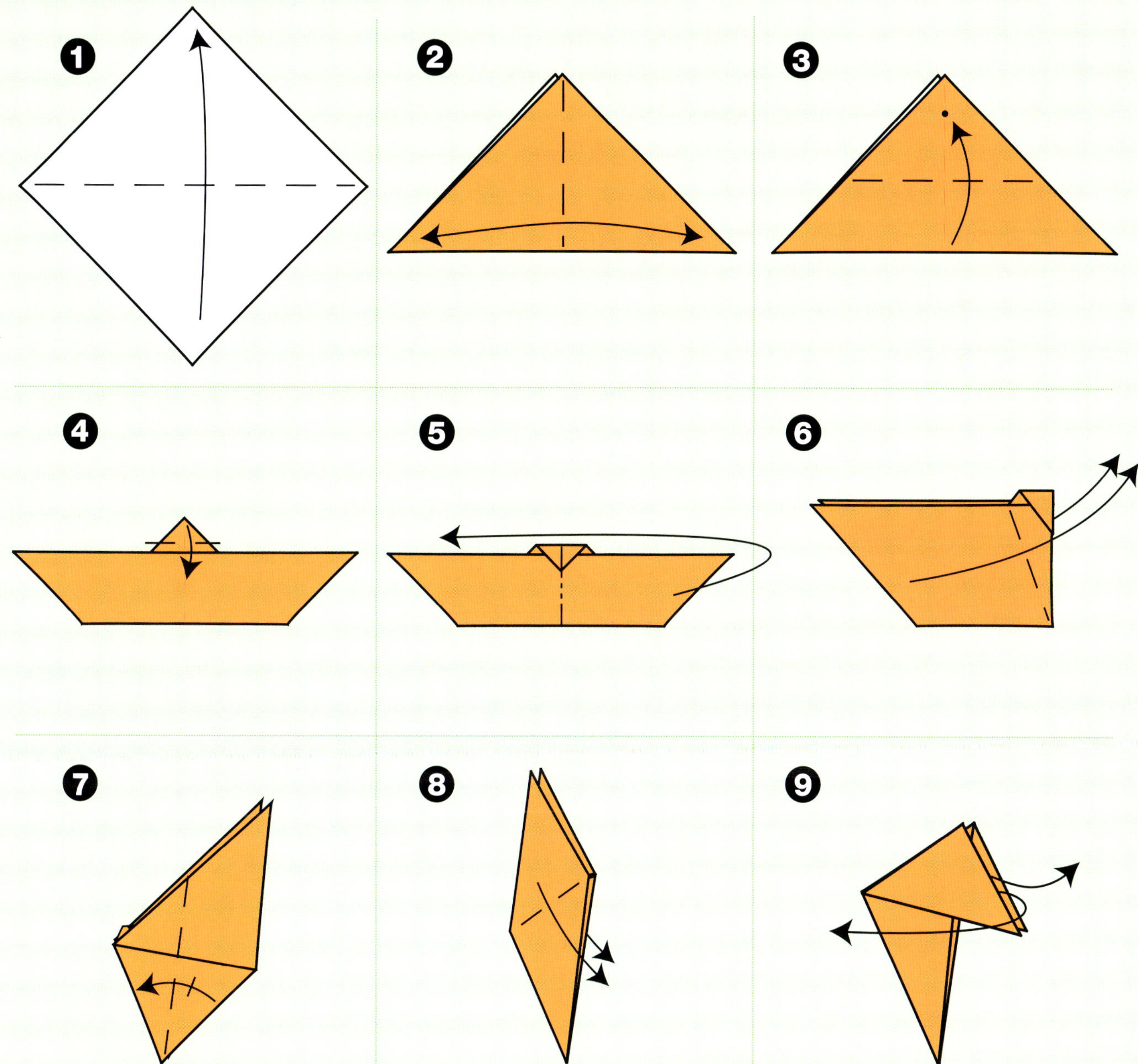
1
2
3
4
5
6
7
8
9

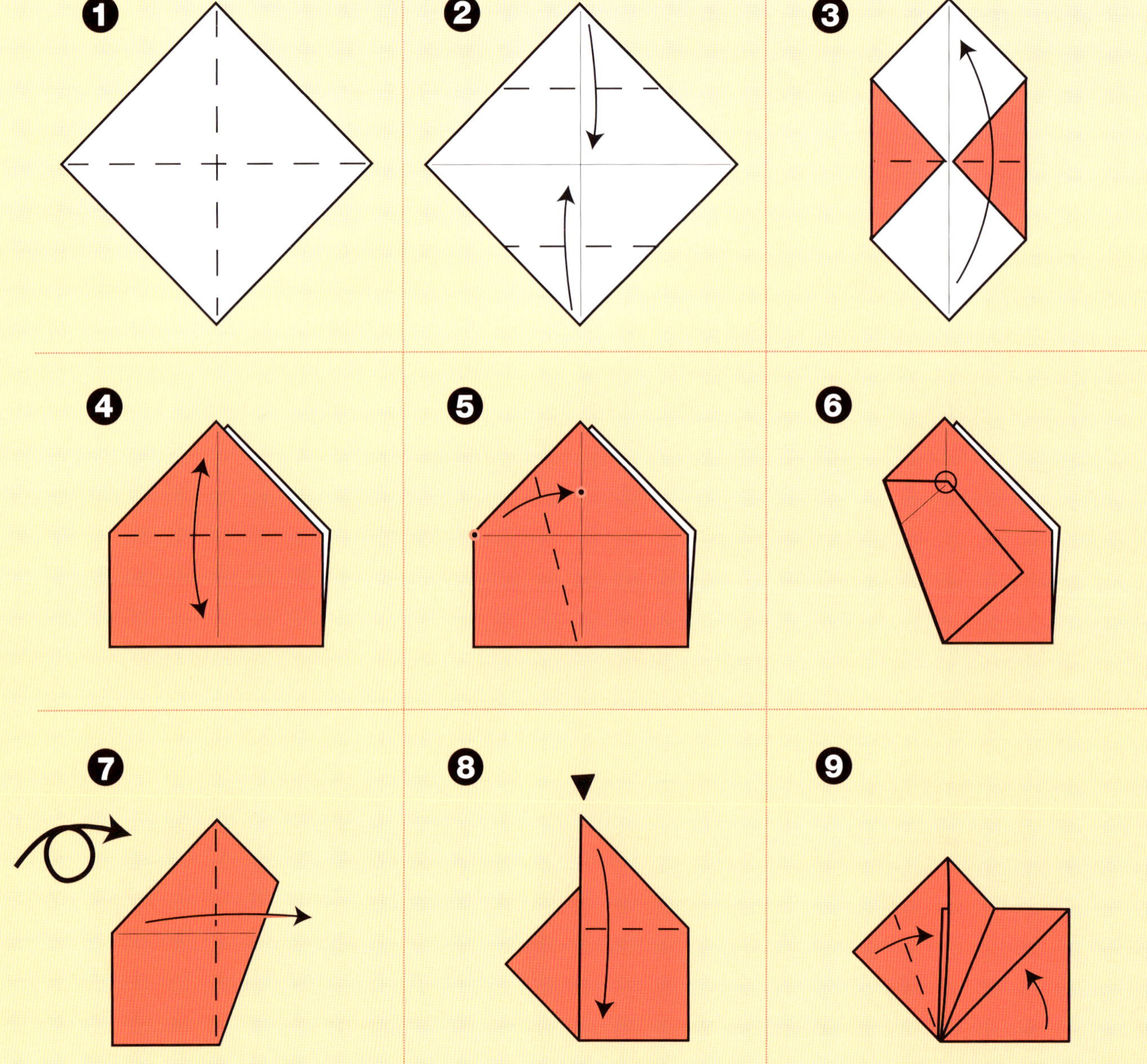
1
2
3
4
5
6
7
8
9

Pocket Heart

This design is by Francis Ow of Singapore, who has designed over 100 origami heart designs. The move in step eight is both unusual and elegant—fold and unfold it until you understand what is happening. When complete, you can tuck this heart in your pocket. Start with a square, red side downward.

1. Fold corner to opposite corner, crease and unfold, both ways.
2. Fold two opposite corners to the center.
3. Fold in half from bottom to top.
4. Fold the upper triangular flap down, through both layers. Crease and unfold.
5. Make a crease starting at the center of the lower edge. Fold over so that the corner lies along the vertical center crease.
6. Like this. Turn the paper over.
7. Swing the left-hand section over to the right.
8. Fold the top point down, carefully and neatly flattening the paper underneath.
9. Fold both lower outside edges to meet the inside edges.
10. Fold the tips of the upper corners in a little, to round them.

Turn over for the complete pocket heart.

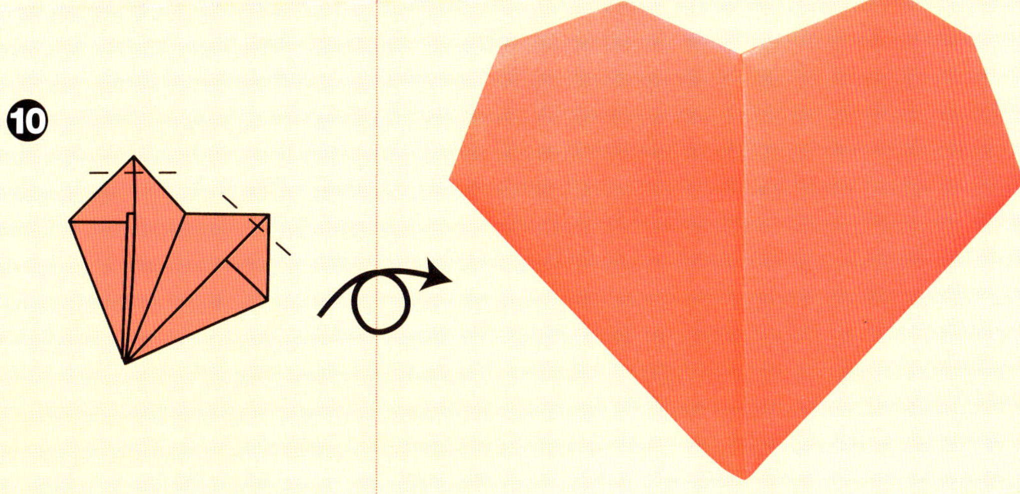

Curvy Dish

This design is by Andrea Crain. She writes about her discovery:
"I was sitting at a conference in Seattle listening to a lecture, and I was absentmindedly playing with a square of paper. I started out making flowers in vases to leave on the conference tables to surprise the cleanup crew. The vase wasn't working out, so I experimented and came up with this!" Some origami creators carefully work out a design before making it, but the majority just play with the paper and see what happens!

1. Start with a square, colored side up. Crease both diagonals.
2. And crease side-to-side both ways.
3. Turn to the white side and fold the lower center-point to touch the upper right diagonal, making sure the crease runs through the center of the paper.
4. Like this—the circled creases should line up. Unfold the paper.
5. Repeat the fold to the right.
6. Mountain-fold the top half of the paper behind.
7. Using existing creases, make a double reverse fold (in and out).
8. Repeat on the other side.
9. Fold up the lower section as far as it will comfortably go.

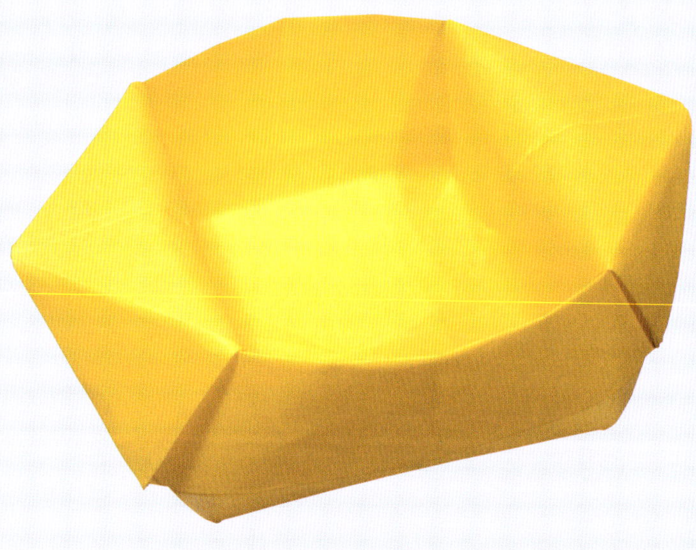

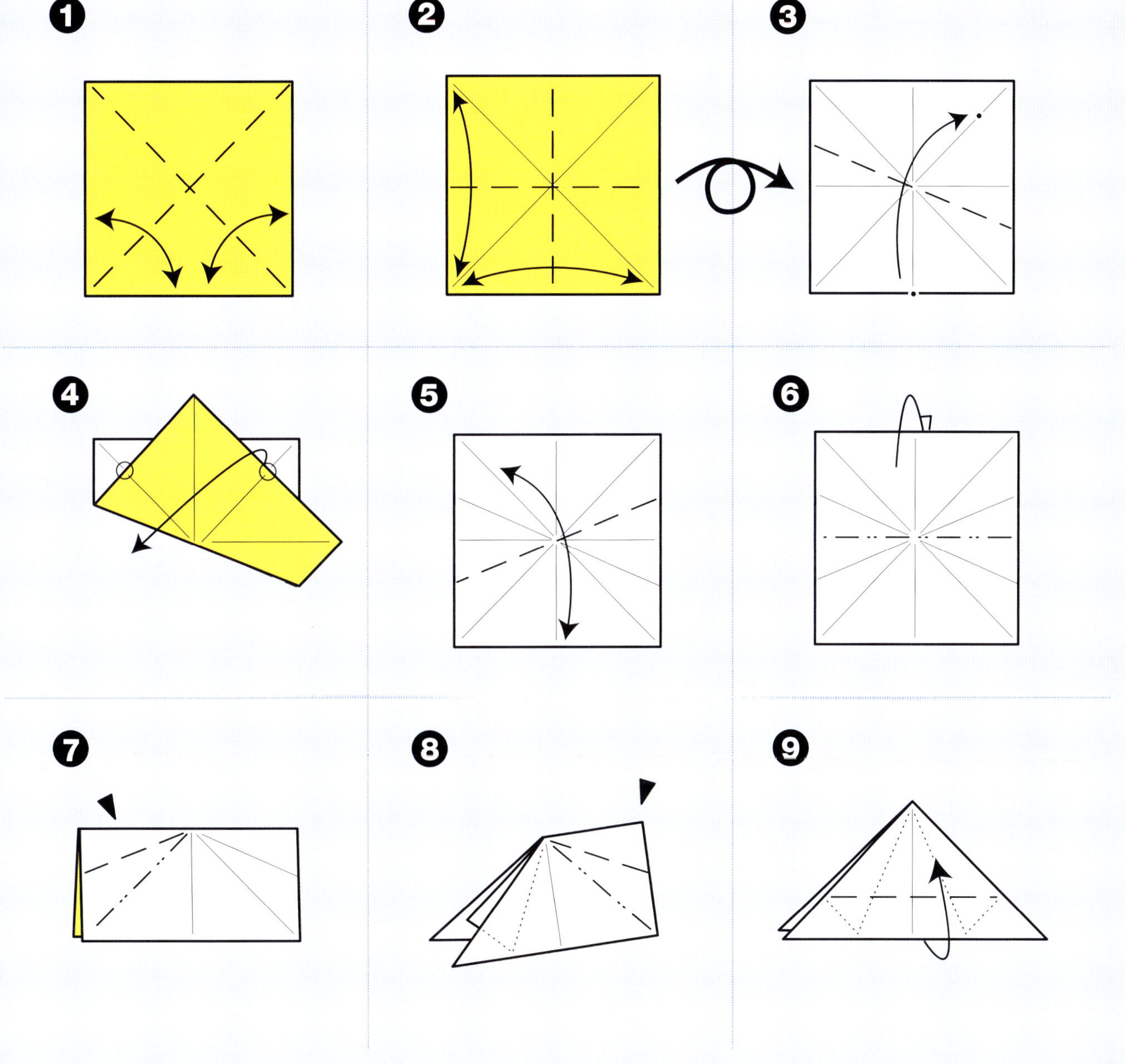

10 Like this. Repeat the fold underneath.

11 Fold the outside corners to meet the inner angle change. Repeat behind.

12 Tuck the white triangles into the pockets, front and back.

13 Make a horizontal valley fold below the colored edge.

14 Open the dish out, changing the last crease into a mountain crease (all the way round) to form the base. Insert your fingers to smooth the dish.

15 Finished.

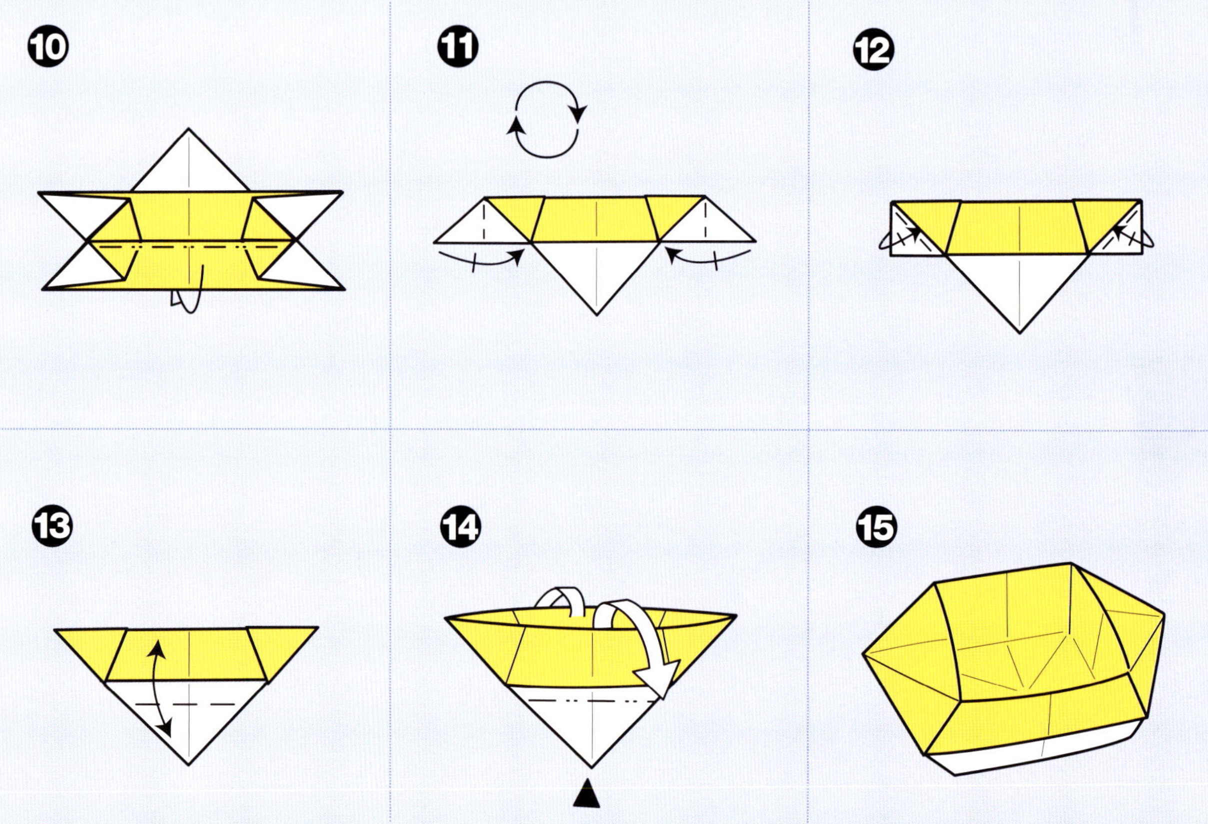

Pencil

A number of designers have come up with this idea. The origami world relies on the honesty of creators to acknowledge where they have made use of someone else's ideas, but it is inevitable that many people create near-identical simple designs independently. As a challenge, think carefully about the final design and see if you can come up with a different sequence to produce the same result.

Start with a rectangle of paper, colored side down. The narrower it is, the longer the pencil will be.

1 Fold the two long sides together, crease and unfold.

2 Fold a corner over to lie along the vertical crease.

3 Like this. Turn the paper over.

4 Fold the circled corners to meet.

5 Fold the right-hand side behind, using the original half-way crease.

6 Shape the point of the pencil with two mountain creases.

Complete.

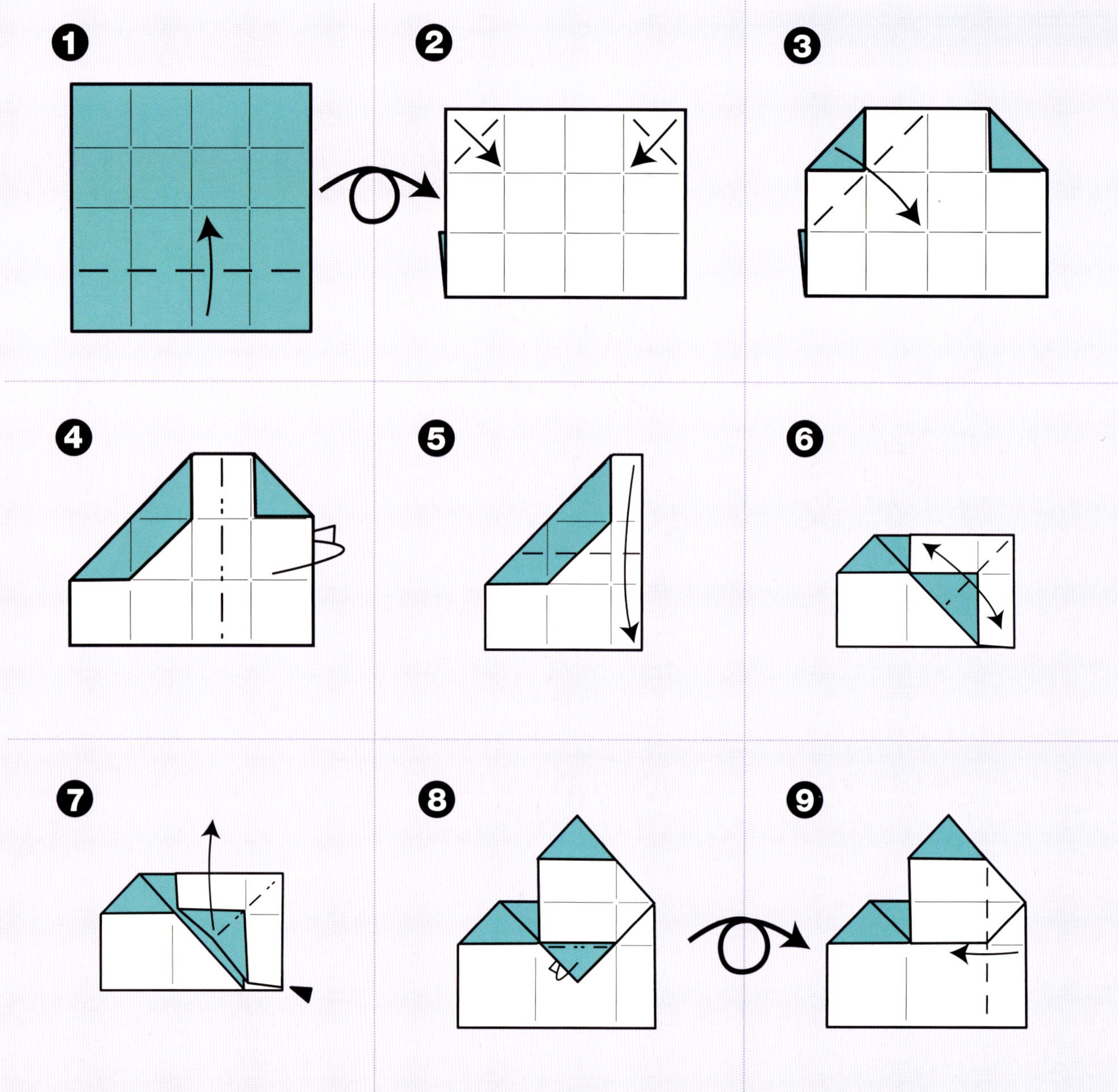
1
2
3
4
5
6
7
8
9

Church

Simple buildings are well suited to origami, since their shape consists mostly of rectangles or triangles. This design by Evi Binzinger makes good use of the different colors on each side of the paper to highlight the roof sections. Start with a square, colored side upward, that has been creased into fourths both ways.

1 Fold over the lower quarter section.

2 Turn the paper over, then fold in the top corners to meet the quarter crease.

3 Fold the upper-left flap over again.

4 Make a mountain fold down the center of the vertical white area. The two upper corners should come together. You can make this more easily as a valley fold from the other side.

5 Take the upper-right corner to the bottom-right corner.

6 Fold the right-hand edge to the top edge, crease, and unfold.

7 Lift and squash fold the flap.

8 Mountain fold the triangular section behind.

9 Fold the right-hand side over on an existing crease. Crease, then unfold half-way to form a stand.

Turn over for the completed church.

Tree

Jason Neale came up with this wonderful tree. The beauty of it (apart from the looks) is that you don't need to be precise with the first three folds. Aim to place them where shown, but if not, you'll simply produce a differently shaped tree! You can add further "shaping" mountain creases at the end if you wish to make it more rounded.

1 Fold the lower-left corner to near the top center. You don't need to be accurate.

2 Like this. Unfold again.

3 Fold the lower corner to the approximate center of the left-hand side.

4 Refold the angled crease, passing it through both layers.

5 Make an inside reverse fold on the corner.

6 Fold over through both layers—the paper becomes 3D.

7 Flatten the paper where it feels most natural.

8 Like this.

9 Turn over for the finished tree.

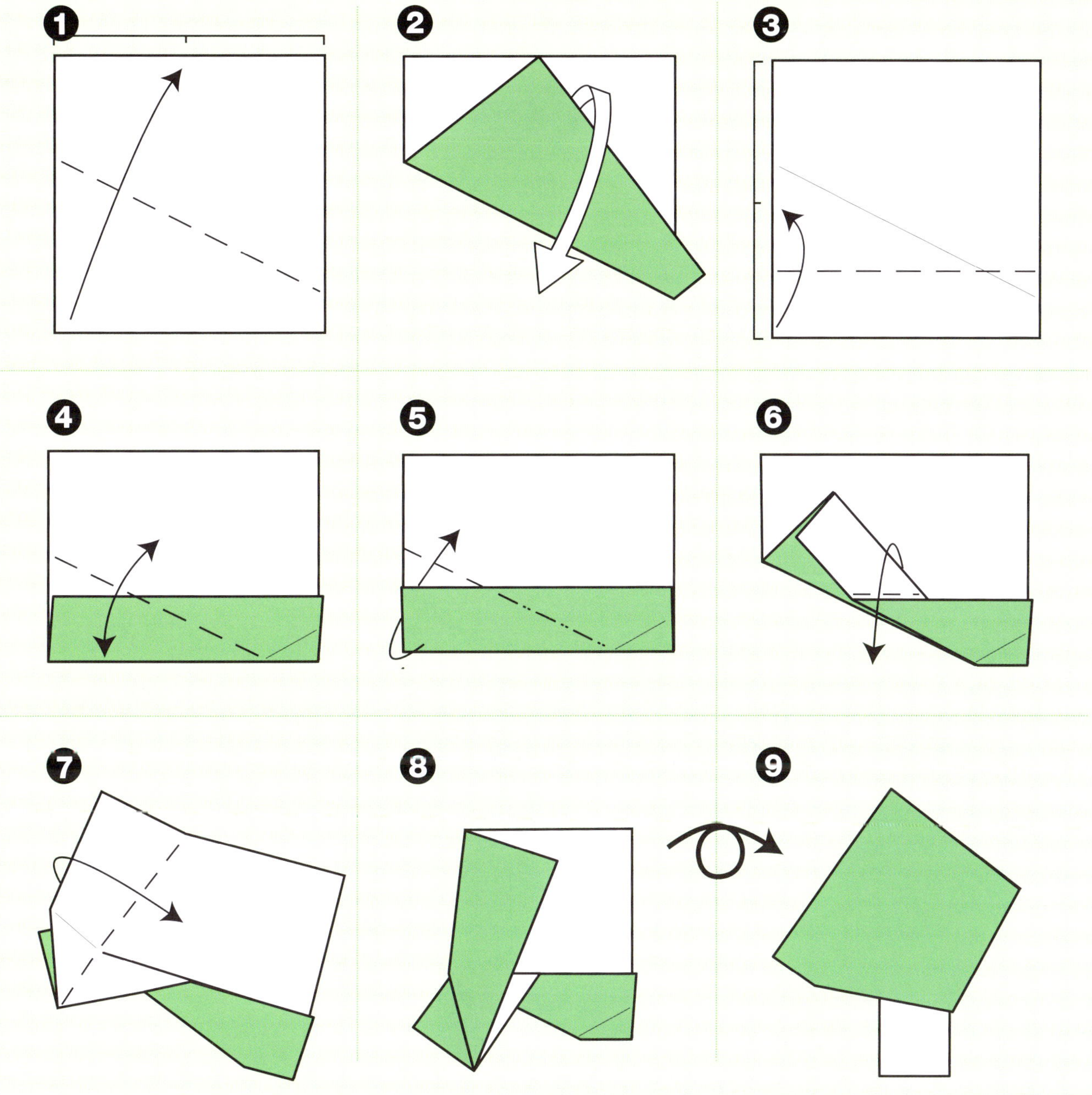
1
2
3
4
5
6
7
8
9

Tarumpty tum tum

This excellent game was created by Siero Takegawa of Japan. The idea is that because one side of it has more layers than the other, it's heavier. This means that if you place it with the sides facing straight forward and the heavy side on top, then gently tip it forward, it will perform a somersault. Demonstrate it working and casually place it with the thin end on top for friends to try. They'll find they can't do it!

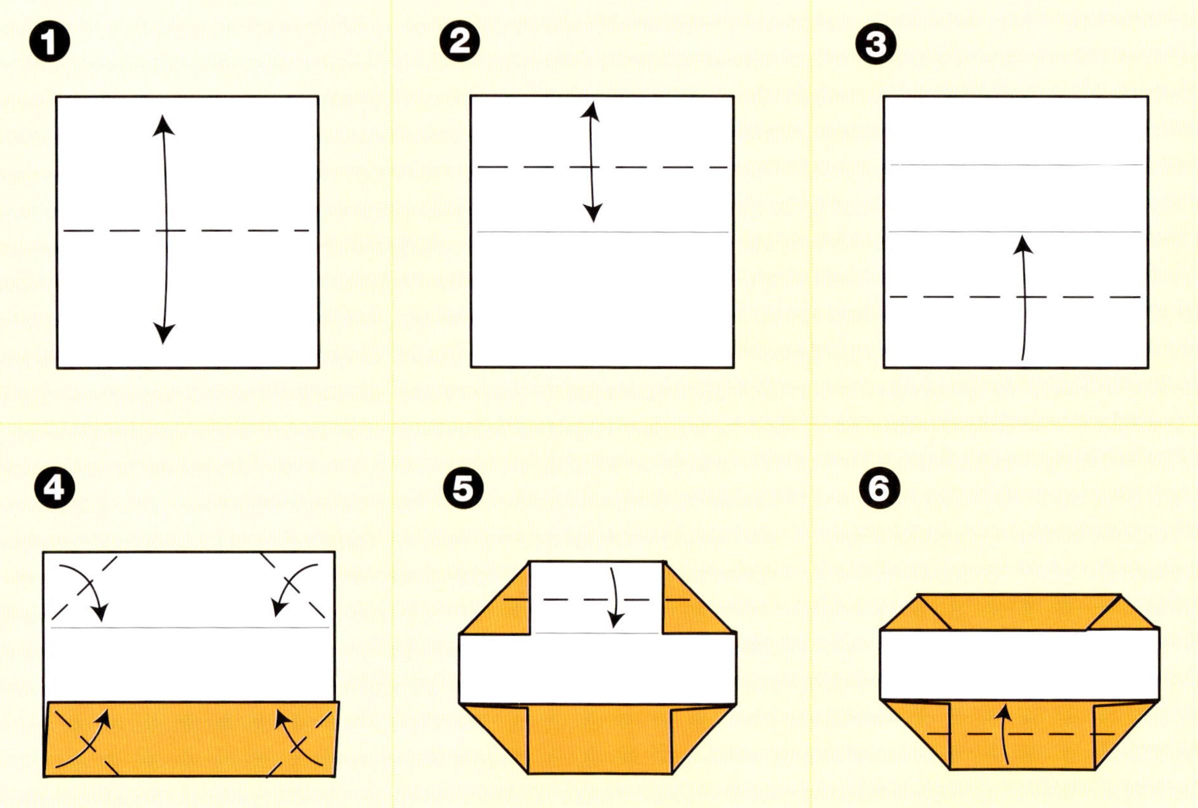

1 Start with a square, white side up. Fold in half, crease, and unfold.

2 Fold the top edge to the center, crease, and unfold.

3 Fold the lower edge to the center.

4 Fold all four corners in—two line up with an edge, the other two with a crease.

5 Fold the upper edge to meet the crease. Try not to let the corners fall out.

6 Repeat with the lower edge.

7 Fold both short edges in to meet (more or less at the center.)

8 Crease them firmly, then open out halfway.

9 Ready to roll!

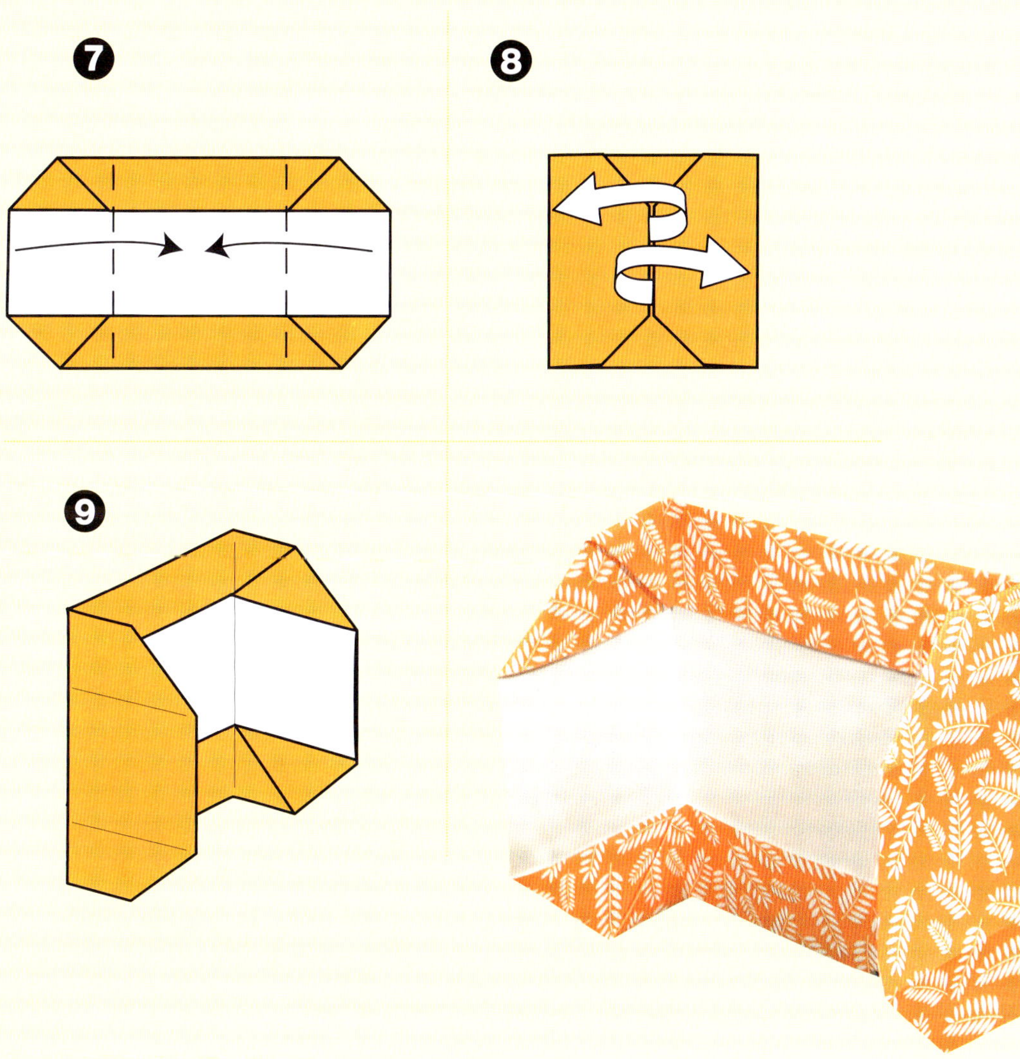

Bowl

Here is a great chance to practice an origami technique known as "pre-creasing." This involves making almost all the creases you need to the flat square before actually folding the model. Once the creases are in place, assembly of the design is much easier. It allows you to be very accurate. This design by the author is heavily influenced by the late Philip Shen, who was creating beautifully elegant dishes as far back as the 1950s.

1 Start with a square, colored side up. Crease both diagonals.

2 Fold the lower-right edge to the horizontal diagonal, but only crease where shown.

3 Rotate the paper 90 degrees anti-clockwise and repeat the step. Continue to add the remaining two creases.

4 Turn the paper over and fold the lower-right edge to the horizontal diagonal, creasing all the way along.

5 Rotate and repeat the fold three times.

6 Turn back to the colored side. Fold the lower corner to the upper corner of the octagonal creases. Only crease where shown. Repeat three more times.

7 Make sure the octagonal pattern is made only of valley creases (four will be mountains).

8 Turn over again. Look for the crease you made in step five, then add a horizontal crease which starts at the lower-left end of that crease. Repeat on each corner.

9 Fold the lower-right raw edge to meet the crease made in the last step, crease, and unfold. Repeat on each corner.

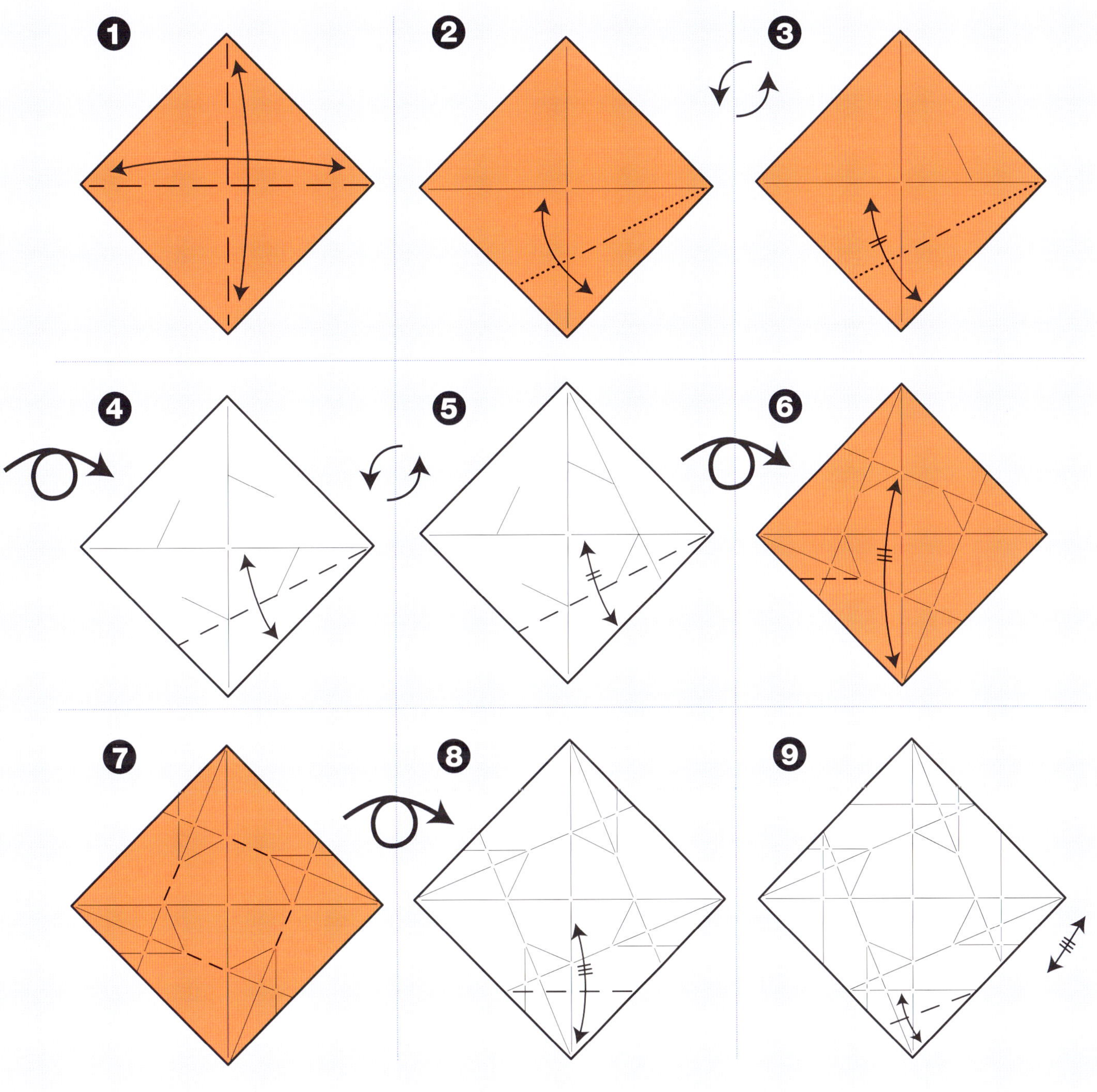
1
2
3
4
5
6
7
8
9

10 OK, now we can start to make the bowl! Put in the lower two creases, encouraging the sides to fold away from you. The octagon creases should be mountains.

11 Fold the lower pointed flap upward and carefully tuck the end behind the white flap, into the pocket formed there.

12 Repeat the move on each corner, then gently firm all creases and press the base from underneath, to create a slight "dimple" in the center.

13 Complete.

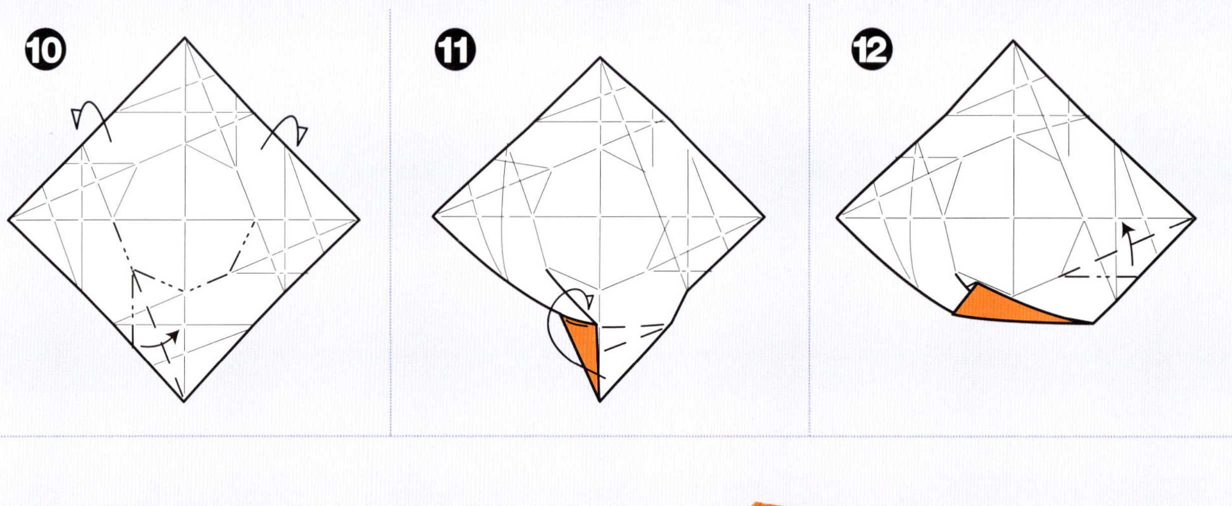

Mammoth

This design by the author is an example of "minimal" folding. The idea is to create a recognizable subject with as few creases as possible. This tends to mean that some folds are made "by eye," in other words, there is no obvious location to fold to. Step 2, for example. The way to approach this is to fold the paper over loosely, then look at it, and adjust until you're happy with how it looks. Start with a square of paper, brown side downward.

1 Fold the top-left corner back along an imaginary diagonal, to a point near the opposite corner.

2 Form the head by folding the top left corner over to the left and slightly down. Compare with the next diagram before flattening the paper.

3 Fold the tip of the tail behind.

4 Fold the white section behind, then open to half way, to form a base.

5 Stand the completed mammoth on the base.

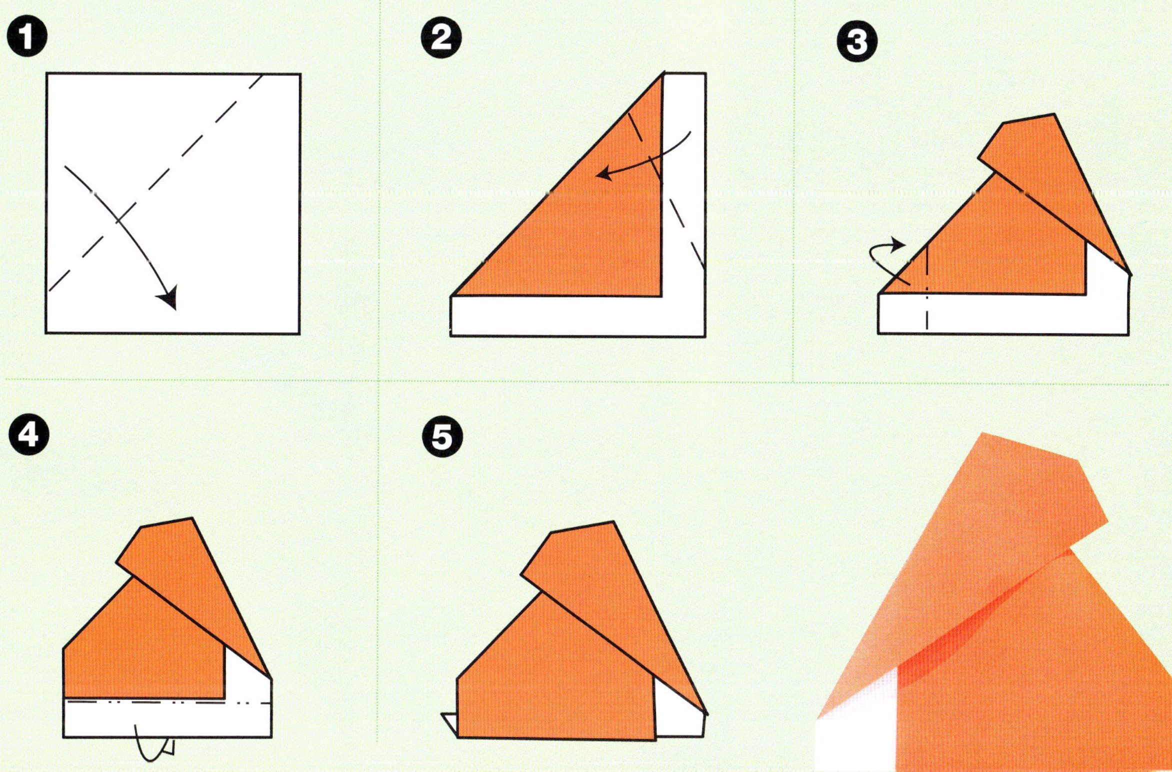

Bench

This is a development of a traditional design (the "house") that goes back many, many years. Most children in Japan are taught to make this while at school. It is part of a sequence of subjects that you can make by adding extra folds to the same starting point. It is a good model to teach people, since it includes a clear example of the "squash" fold.

1. Start with a square, white side up. Fold in half from side to side, crease, and unfold.
2. Fold in half from top to bottom.
3. Fold the short sides in to the center.
4. (Enlarged view) Fold the upper edges to lie on the outer edges, crease and unfold.
5. Open the upper layer as far as it will go, carefully squashing the colored section into a neat triangle.
6. Repeat on the other side.
7. This is the traditional "house". Fold the central section up to the top edge.
8. Fold the sides in on existing creases. Make these crease very firm.
9. Hold the section that you folded up in step seven, then ease it down. Allow the side flaps to open. When it's just past half way, let go. The tension of the paper should hold it in place.

   Complete.

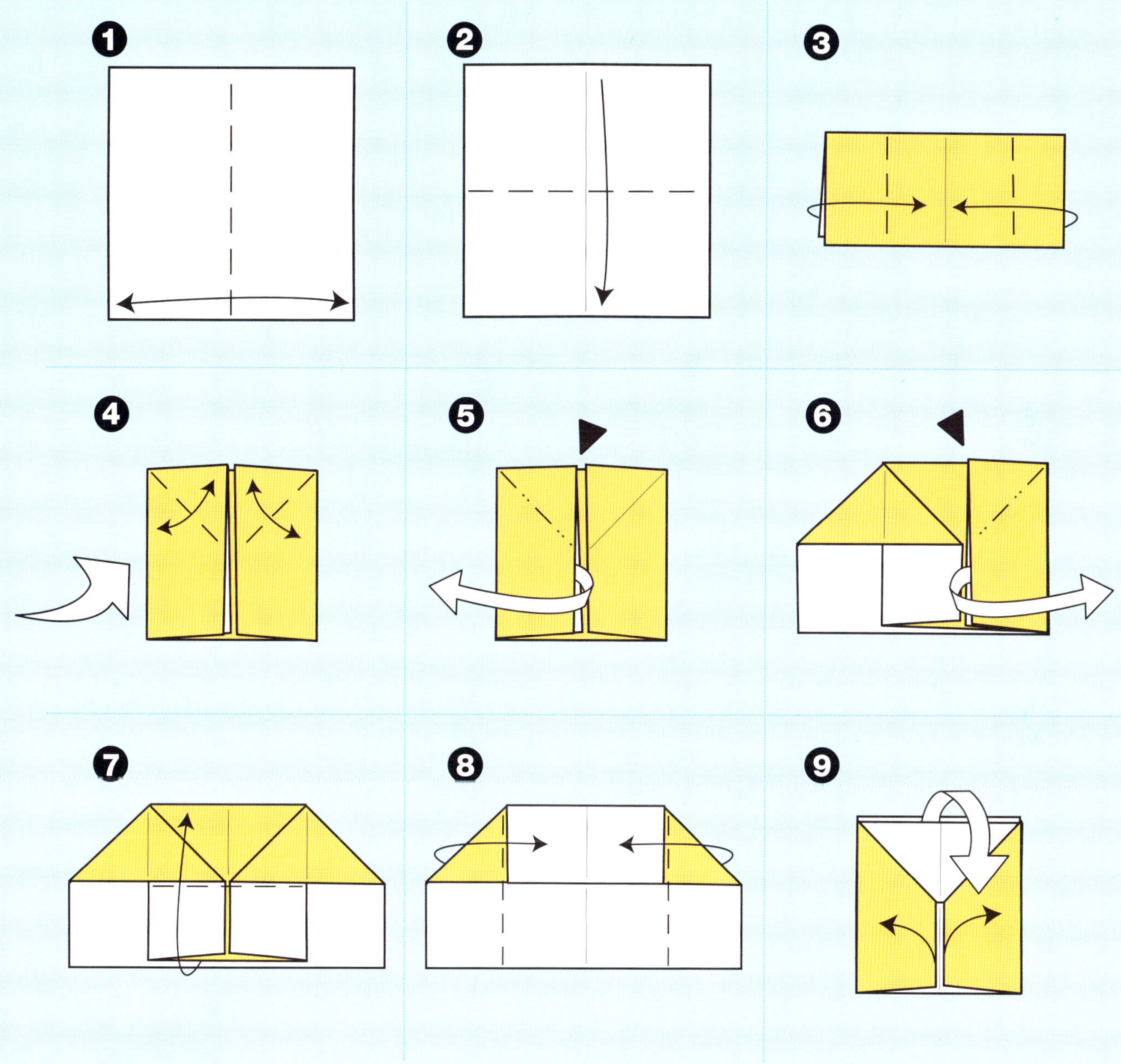
1
2
3
4
5
6
7
8
9

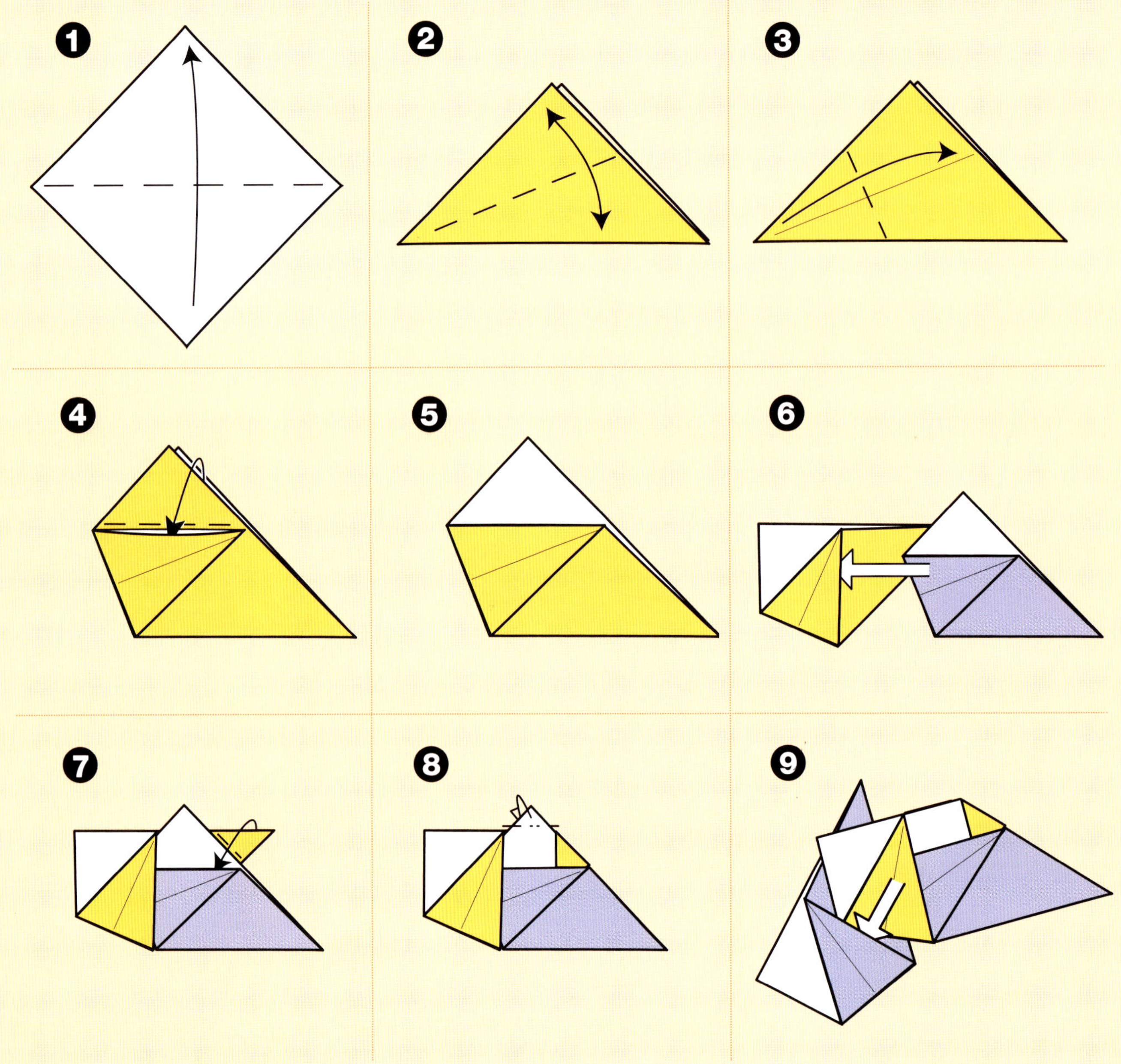
1
2
3
4
5
6
7
8
9

Modular Ring

Modular origami makes use of simple "units" which join together to form more complex forms. Some are 3D, many are flat, and form rings or wreaths. This design was discovered by Kuni Kasahara (amongst others). To make it look really attractive, you should try to be as accurate as you can when creasing. If your folding is sloppy, it will look poor and won't hold together well.

1 Start with a square, colored side down. Fold in half from bottom to top.

2 Fold the top left layer of paper over to meet the lower edge. Crease and unfold.

3 Fold the left-hand corner to the end of the crease.

4 Tuck the upper triangular flap into the pocket below it.

5 This is the result. Make another seven, using alternating colors.

6 Slide one unit into the other as shown here.

7 Fold the small point from underneath into the small pocket.

8 Now fold the top triangular flap over and into a pocket.

9 Add the remaining units in the same way, working in an anti-clockwise direction.

10 You can join seven units by raising the ring into 3D—this makes a brilliant spinner!

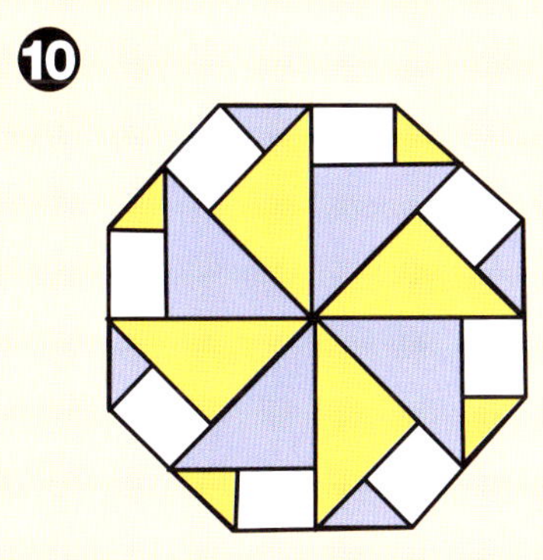

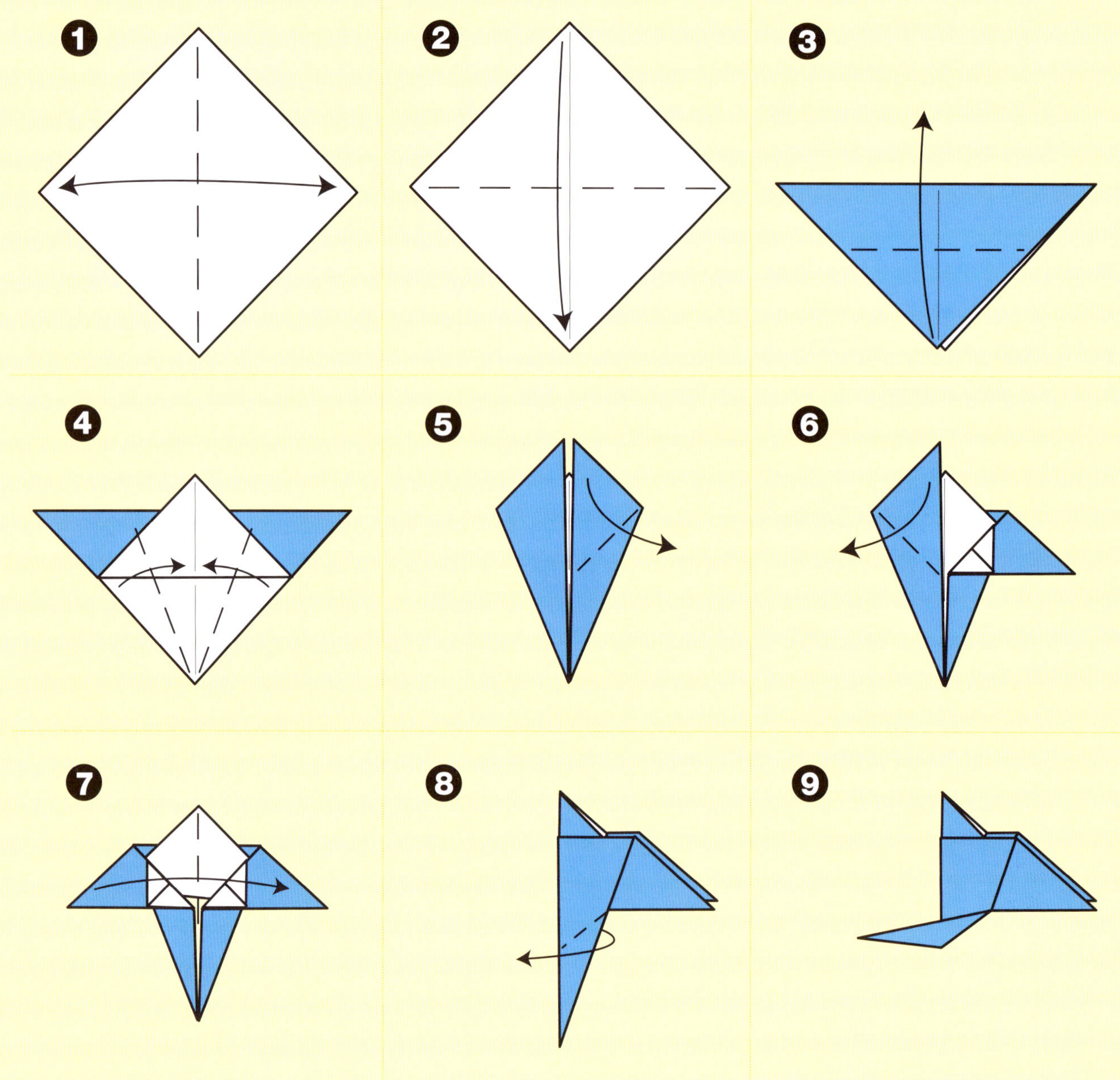

1
2
3
4
5
6
7
8
9

Hummingbird

John Smith is a folder who has a special approach to designing—he only uses simple valley or mountain folds, no sinks, squashes, or reverses. He calls this approach "Pureland" and feels it encourages designers to capture a design as simply as possible. This hummingbird is a fine example—see how in steps 7 and 9 he finds an alternative to what would usually be a reverse fold.

1. Start with a square, colored side down. Fold in half from side-to-side, crease, and unfold.
2. Fold in half from top to bottom.
3. Fold the lower point back up, so it folds past the edge a little.
4. Fold the raw white edges to meet the vertical center crease.
5. Fold the right-hand flap over at right angles.
6. Like this. Repeat on the left-hand side.
7. Fold the model in half from left to right.
8. Fold the sharp point to the left.
9. Like this. Turn the paper over.
10. Narrow the beak by folding it in half.
11. Complete.

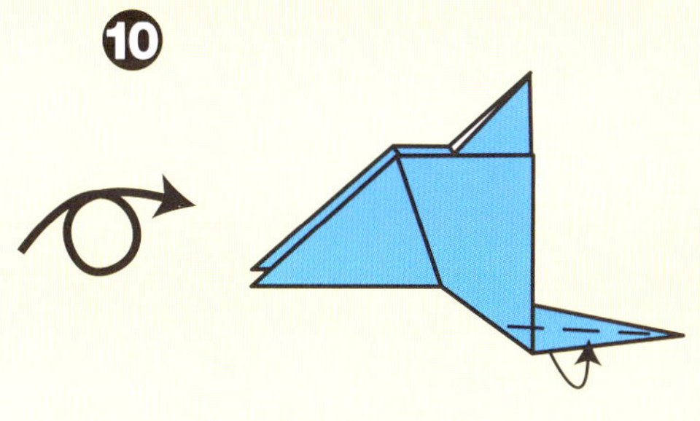

Beaky

Using a rectangle of paper makes it possible to explore ideas away from traditional bases and geometry. This sequence, while unusual, uses the natural angles of the paper to produce a clean, flowing sequence. It's also what is known as an "action" model—in other words, it does something! Hold the paper on either side of the eyes and work your hands in-and-out a little—the beak will open and close!

1. Start with a rectangle of paper, in this case a sheet of letter paper. Fold in half both ways.
2. Fold all four corners in toward the center crease.
3. Fold in half from bottom to top.
4. Fold the left-hand corner over, making the crease pass through the upper-left corner.
5. Fold the flap back so that the crease starts where the flap meets the vertical center.
6. Like this. Unfold the flap and repeat on the right-hand side.
7. Inside-reverse both flaps—you'll need to make sure the same creases are in place on both sides. Go steady!
8. This is the result. Fold the upper-right corner over—this should feel natural!
9. Fold a layer over the triangular flap, squashing the top point. Check the next step for guidance.
10. Like this. Pull the paper out to hide the lower half of the squashed flap.
11. Repeat the last three steps on the other side.
12. Open the paper from either side, forming it into the finished beak.

    Complete.

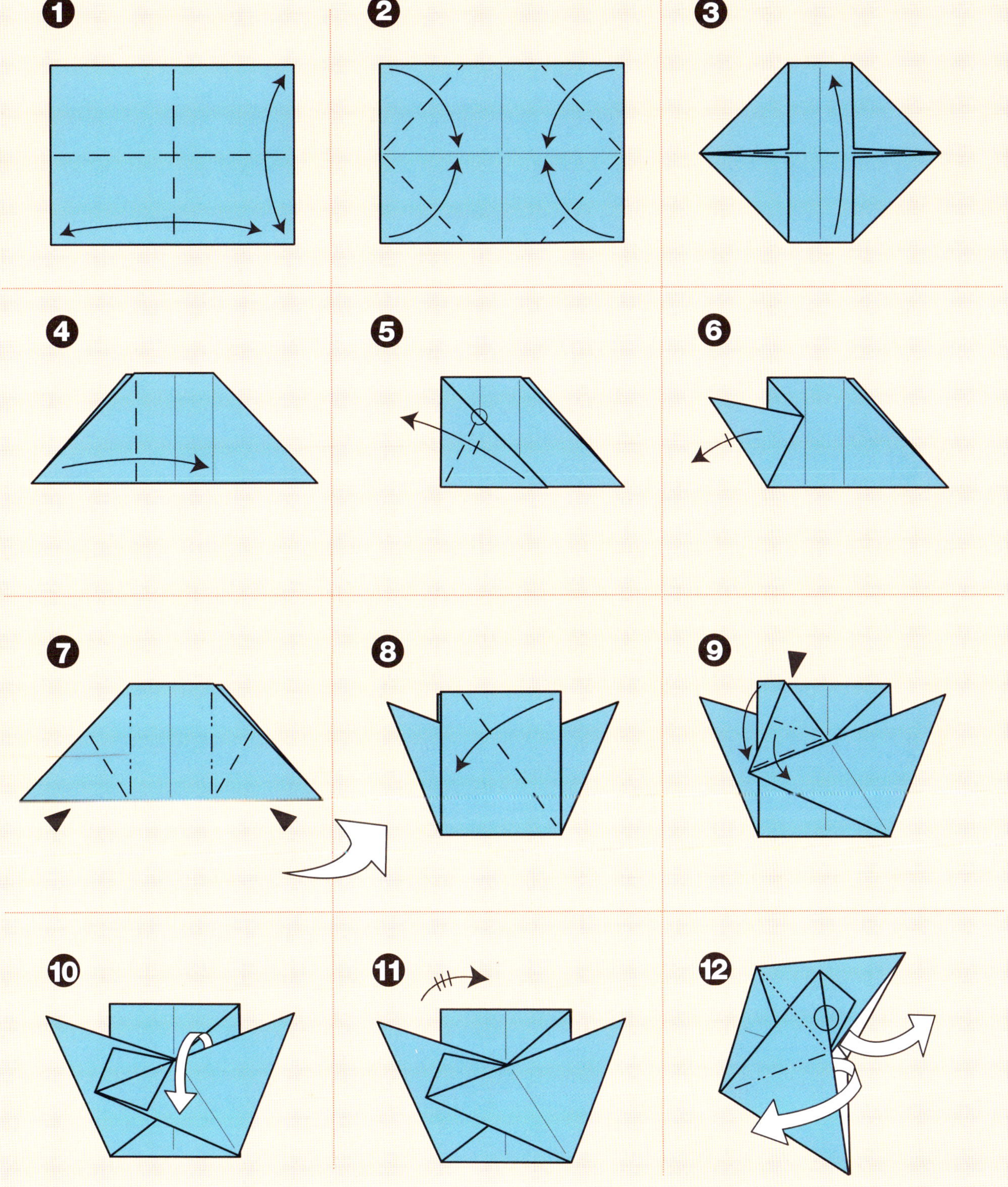
1
2
3
4
5
6
7
8
9
10
11
12

"Pureland" Fish

Marc Kirschenbaum is an American folder noted for his complex designs, yet he can also turn his hand to the opposite end of the complex spectrum, as shown by this "pureland" (i.e. only valley and mountain folds) Fish. Offsetting the initial "fold in half" crease is the key to this design, cleverly producing the lower "lip" of the fish. The design is also exciting because you can't see what you've made until the final turn over step.

1 Start with a square, colored side down. Fold over as if folding in half, but tilt the angle slightly. See the next drawing as a guide.
2 This is the aim. Crease and unfold.
3 Fold the lower-right edge to meet the crease.
4 Refold on the existing crease.
5 This is the result, turn the paper over.
6 Fold the lower-left corner to the upper-right.
7 Fold the top (raw) layer over to meet the short folded edge.
8 Like this.
9 Turn over for the completed fish!

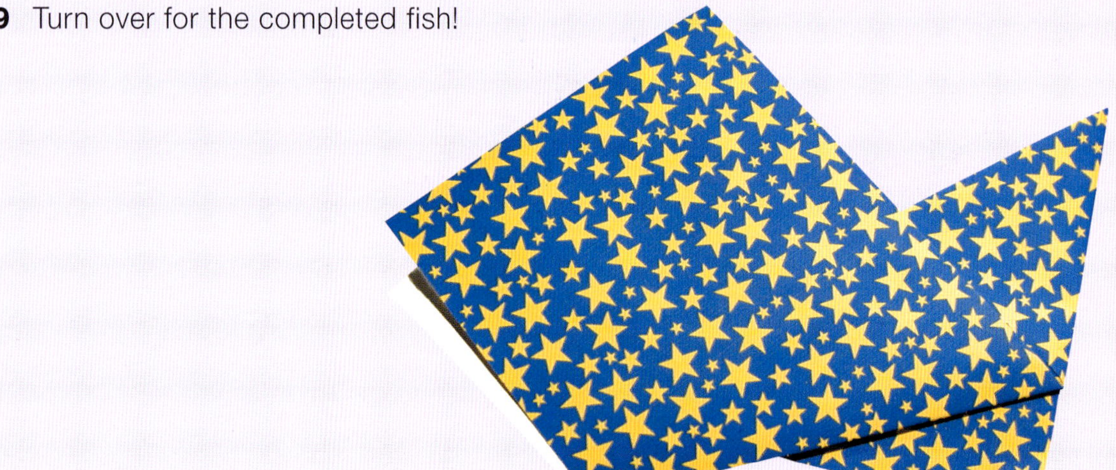

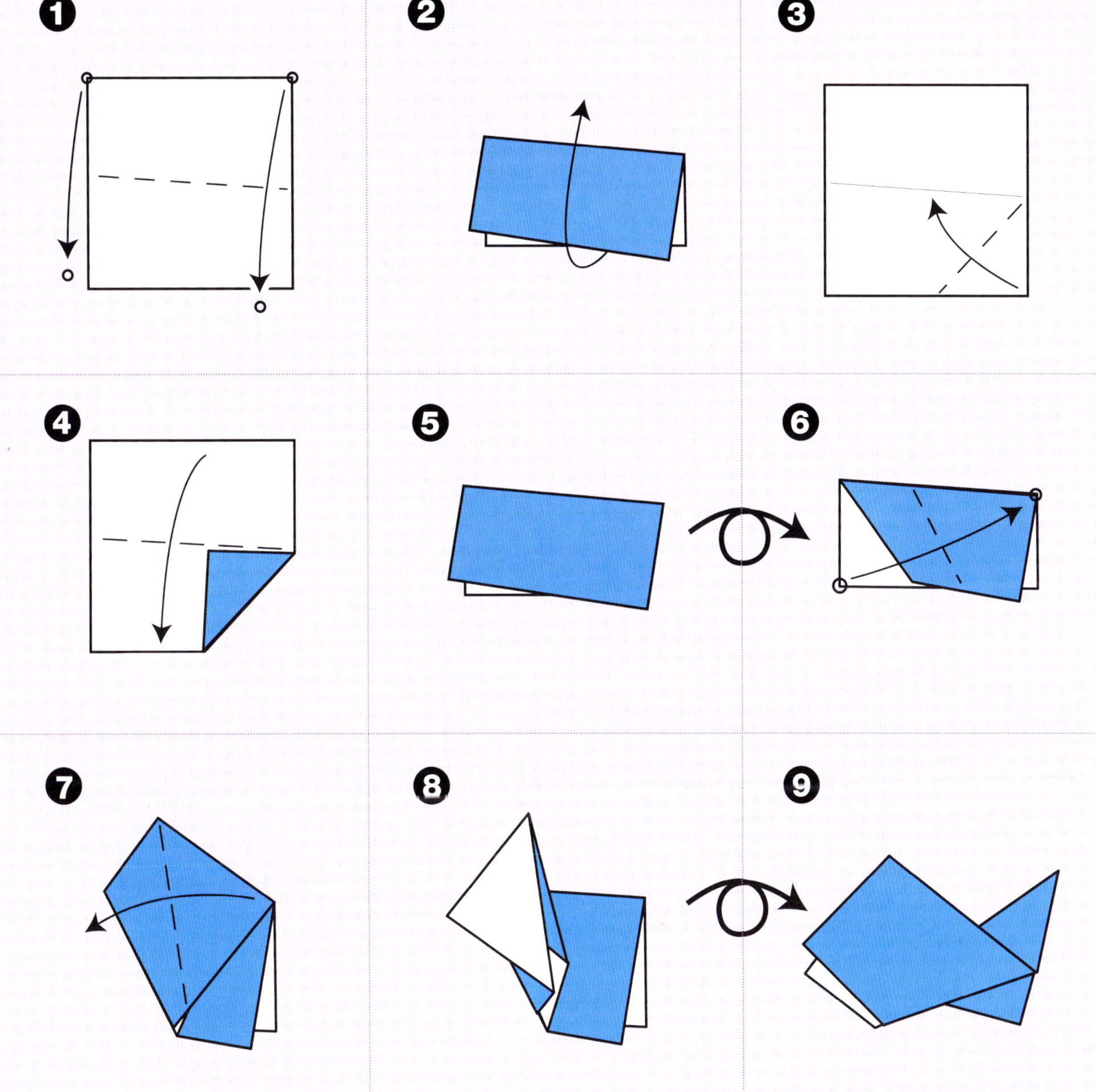
1
2
3
4
5
6
7
8
9

Frog

Here's another simple animal's head, this time, a frog. The creases also allow you to make the frog "talk" if you gently press the sides of the head together. The squash fold at step 6 is a very useful technique. More experienced folders often make the squash without the pre-crease made in step 5, but beginners should always add the crease before squashing. Start with a square of paper, colored side upward.

1. Fold side to side, crease and unfold, both ways.
2. Turn the paper over and rotate it, to make the next step easier. Fold corner to opposite corner, crease, and unfold.
3. Fold opposite corners in to the center.
4. Fold in half from side to side.
5. Fold the right-angled corners in to touch the crease.
6. Enlarged cut-away view. Lift the small flap so it points upward.
7. Carefully squash the paper symmetrically using the existing crease.
8. Like this. Repeat with the matching corner.
9. Complete.

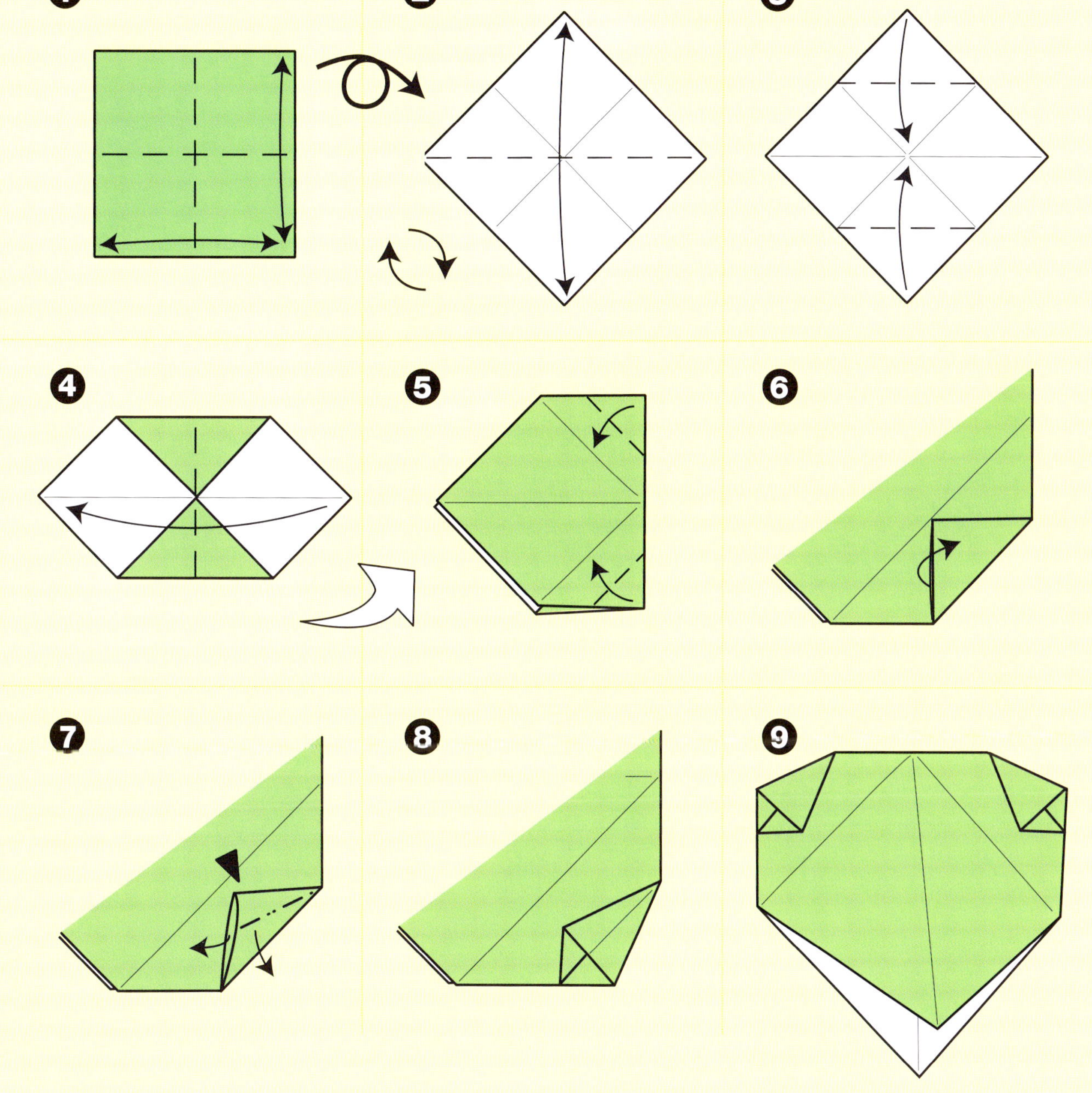
1
2
3
4
5
6
7
8
9

Dinosaur

As with all creative arts, there is a full spectrum from simple to complex. There are many highly complex and realistic origami dinosaurs, but they need a lot of folding ability to complete. This "fin-back" dinosaur is more stylized, but still recognizable. Start with a 2 x 1 rectangle (half a square) with the (dinosaur) colored side downward.

1 Fold in half from top to bottom.

2 Fold the lower edge to the top, repeating the fold underneath - the small dash on the arrow indicates this.

3 Fold the same edge back down in half, on both sides.

4 Fold the short edges to the lower edges, crease and unfold.

5 Inside-reverse fold the corners using the creases you've just made.

6 Swing the flap downward. Repeat the last two steps underneath.

7 Fold the two upper corners to meet in the middle of the lower crease.

8 Like this. Turn the paper over.

9 Make a series of closely-spaced creases to represent the fins.

10 Fold back the lower flap in each side.

11 Fold the right-hand legs over at a slight forward angle, then fold the left-hand legs all the way over.

12 Make the front legs match the rear legs.

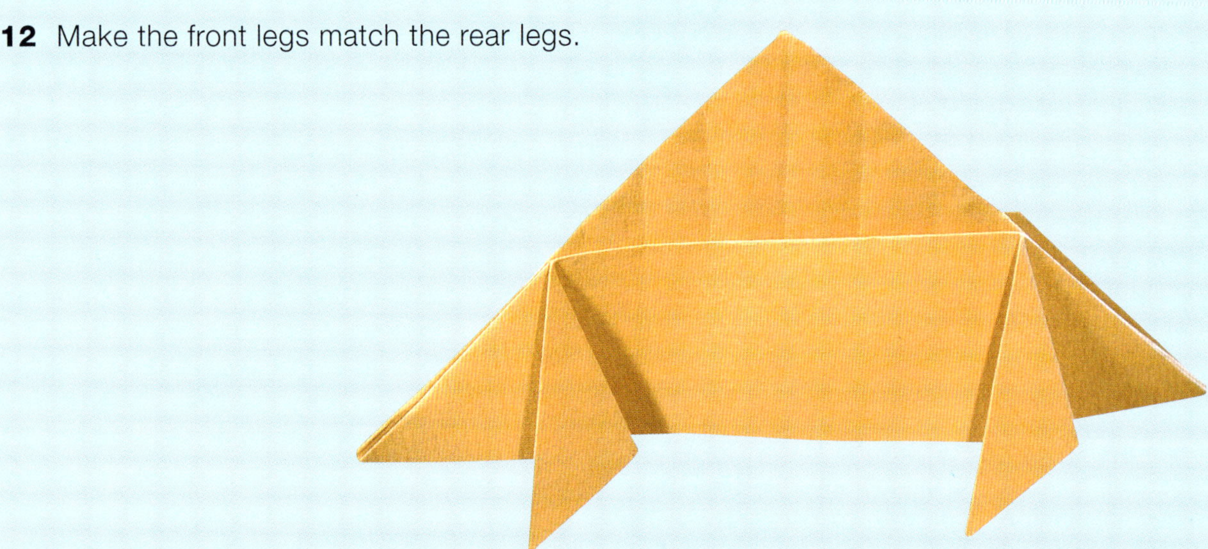

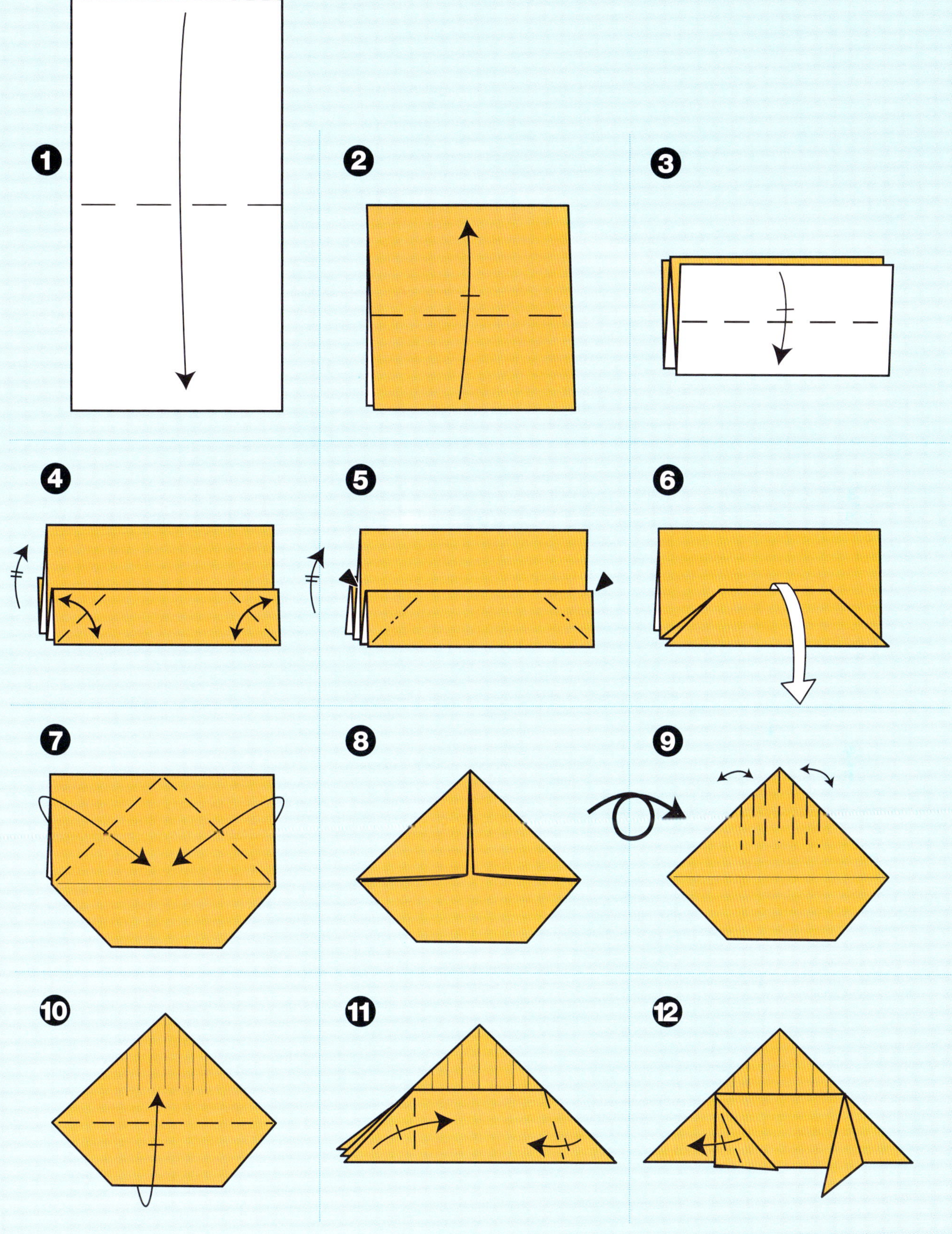
1
2
3
4
5
6
7
8
9
10
11
12

Chickens

Kunihiko Kasahara is one of the world's most gifted creators. He always finds a prefect balance between realism and character. This "rooster" is a perfect example—easily recognizable, yet full of character, and with a clean form. The creator has produced a variation to make a "hen"—you simply adapt a couple of the folding steps.

1. Start with a square, creased corner-to-corner both ways. Fold the left corner to the center.
2. Like this. Turn the paper over.
3. Fold each half of the left-hand edge to meet the horizontal center.
4. Fold the small colored square in half.
5. Leave a small gap, then fold the point out again.
6. Pull the white paper carefully out, flattening it where it seems natural. Repeat on the matching flap.
7. Fold the model in half.
8. This is the result. Let's enlarge the view of the head.
9. Carefully pull up the back of the head, allowing the creases to adjust. Flatten the paper in the new position.

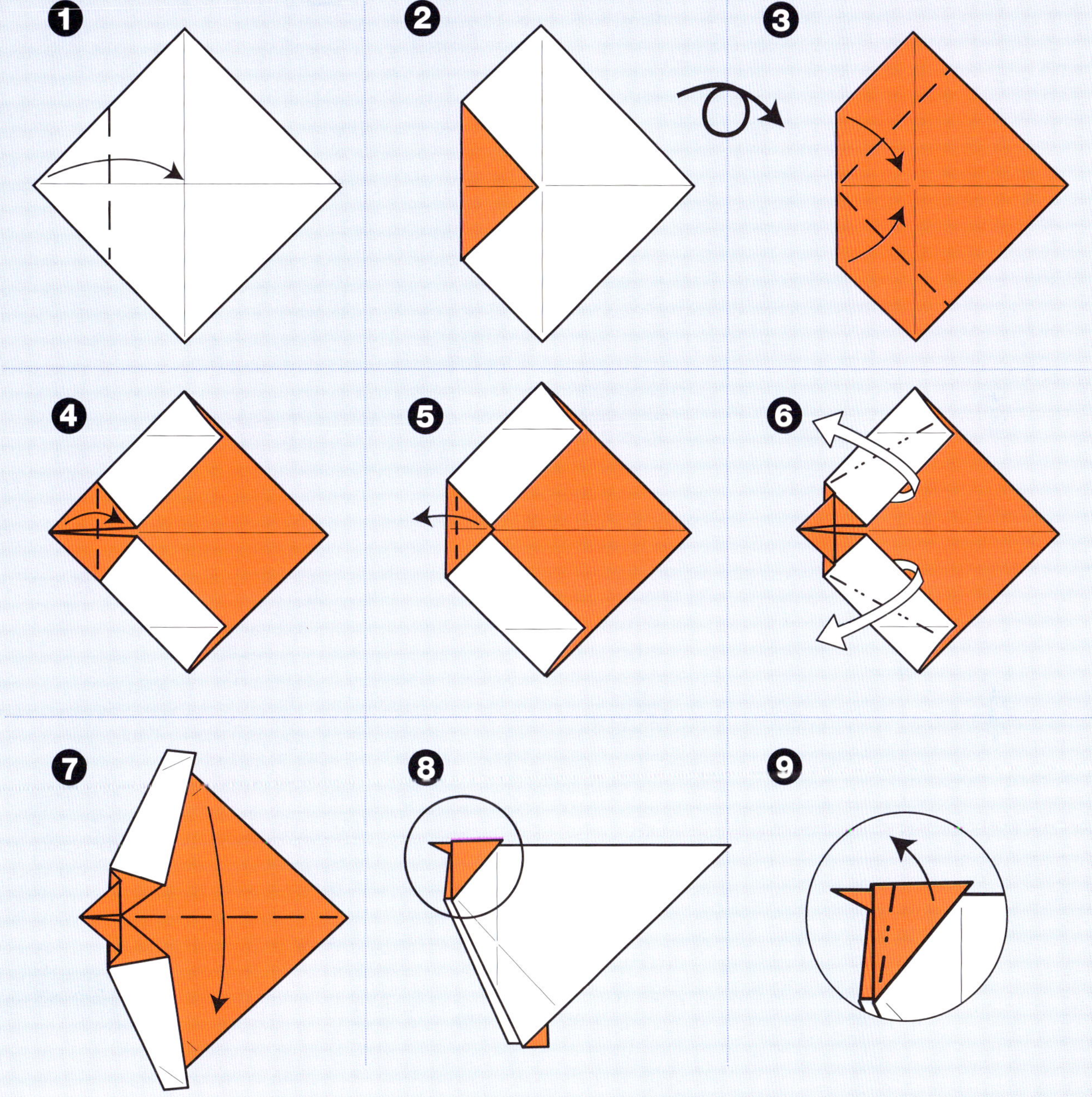
1
2
3
4
5
6
7
8
9

10 Inside reverse the large point.

11 Pull the beak down and flatten it. Reverse fold the tail back up.

13 Fold the lower flaps inside to form the base.

13 Complete!

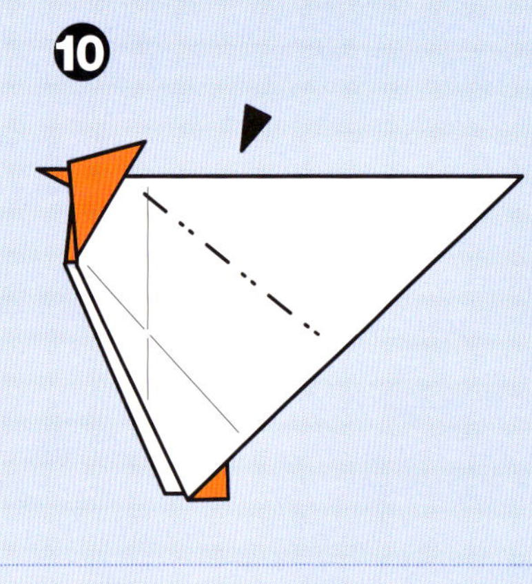

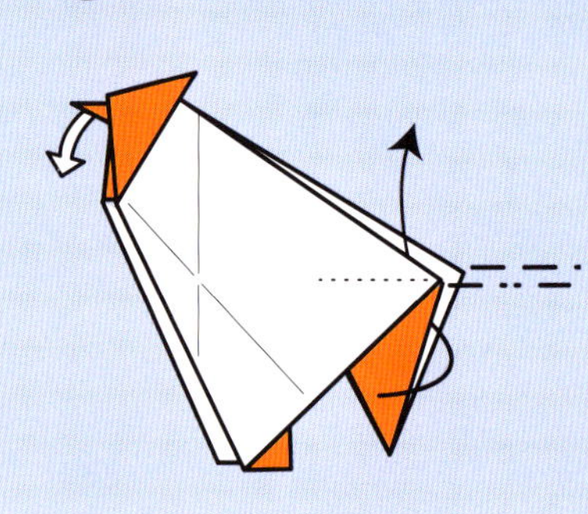

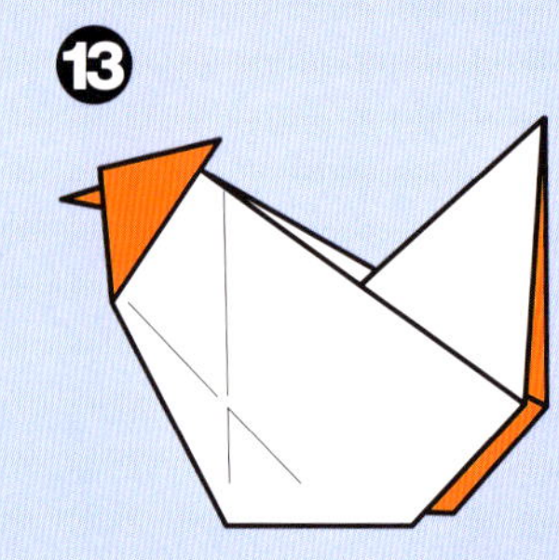

10a To make the Hen, make the reverse fold at a different position.

11a Pull the beak down and flatten it. Reverse fold the tail back up.

12a Make the body shorter by folding more paper in.

13a Hen complete.

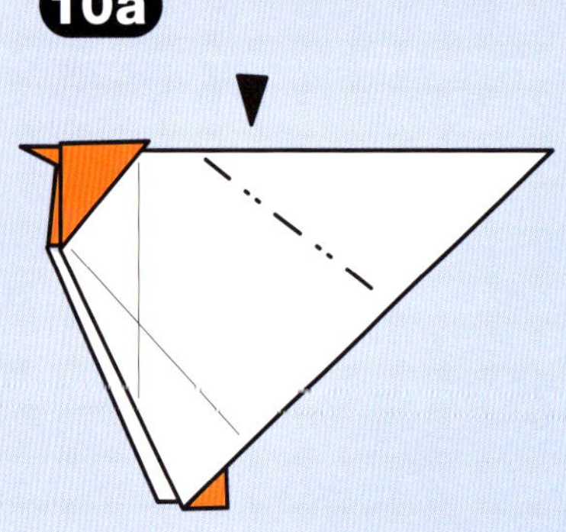

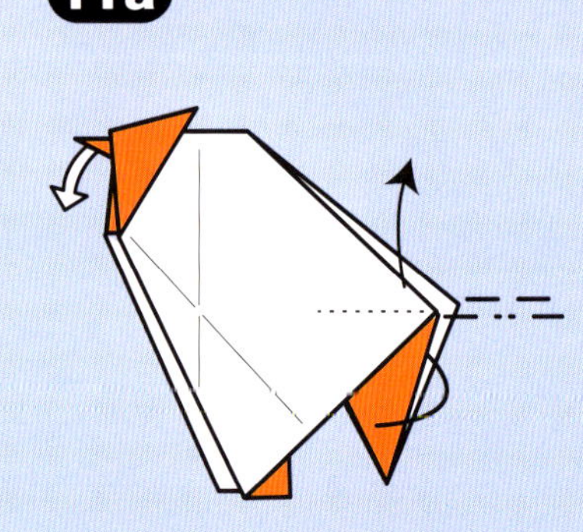

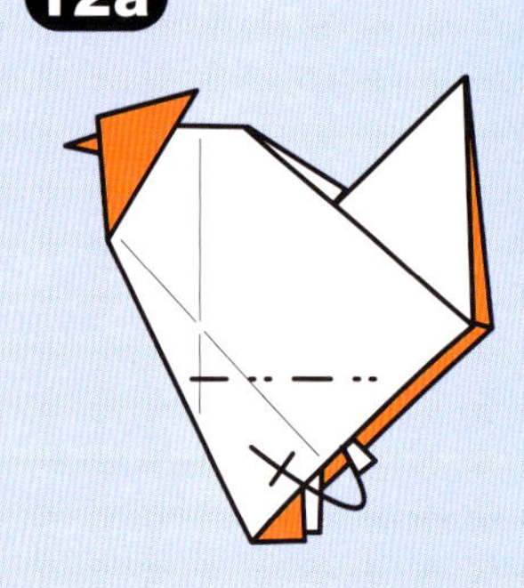

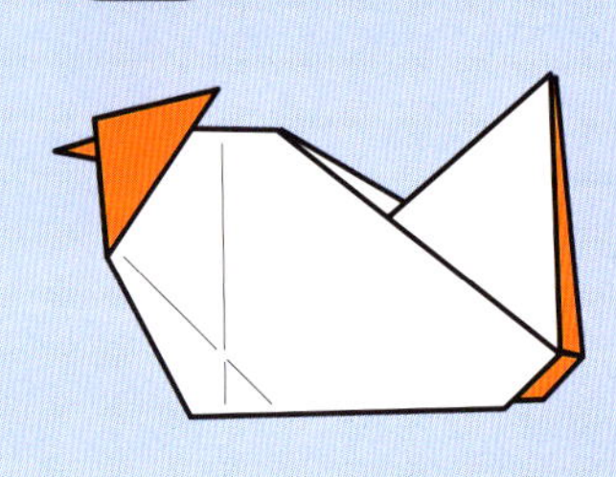

Rose bowl

Like many creators, there are subjects that I keep returning to. One of these is bowls and dishes. I'm always searching for simpler or more elegant ways of making a container. This design arose from an earlier one—I started with an existing crease pattern and made some creases go "the other way"—it soon fell into place.

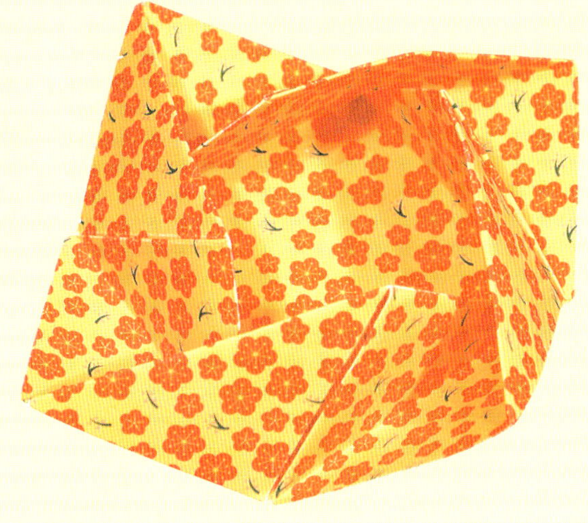

1 Start with a square colored side up. Fold side to side both ways.

2 Turn the paper over and add quarter creases all round.

3 Turn back over and fold corner as shown, creasing only where shown. Repeat on each corner.

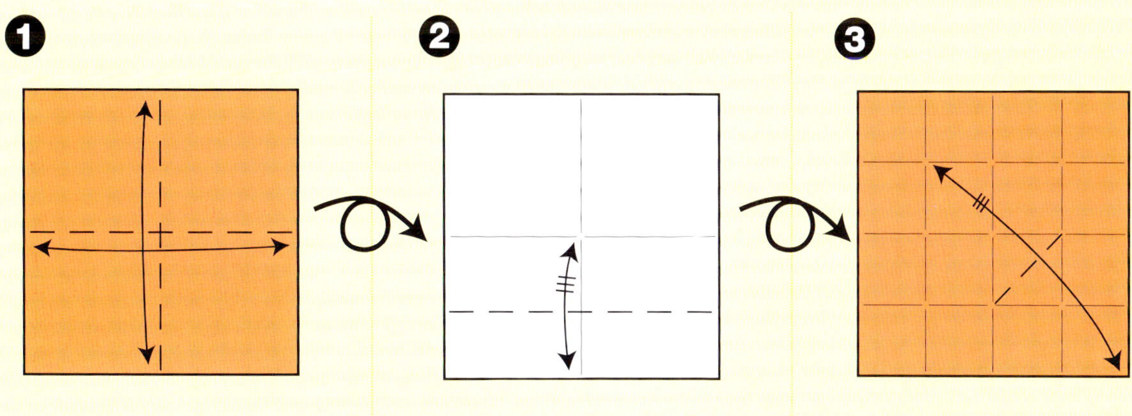

4 Using the creases shown, twist the paper. and collapse into a smaller square.

5 Here's the move in progress…

6 …and complete (the view is enlarged). Fold each top layer corner to the center, crease and unfold.

7 Fold the double layer in half at each corner.

8 Use the creases shown to "swivel" the corner underneath its neighbor.

9 Here's the completed move with the layers opened to show how they lie. Repeat the move on each corner.

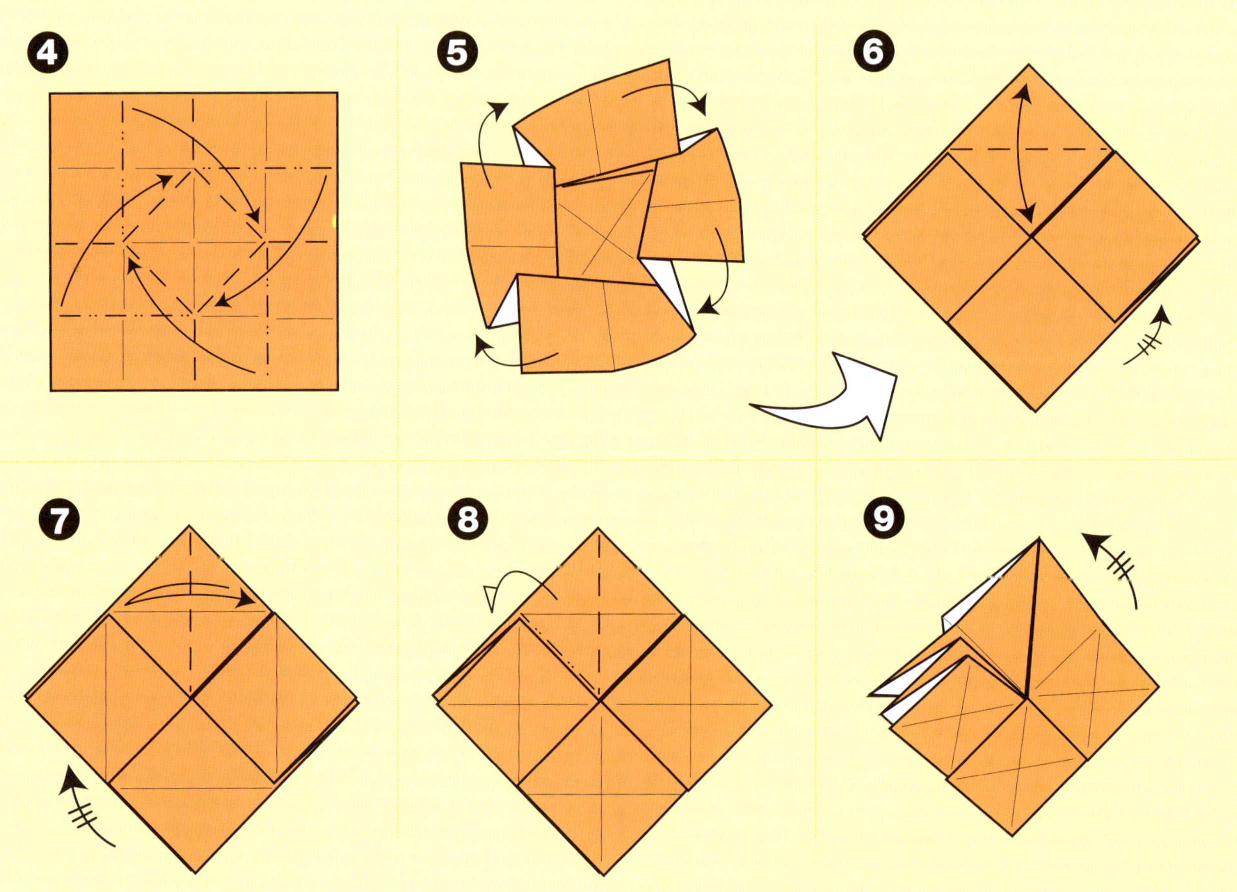

10 All four corners completed. Turn the paper over.

11 Fold the smaller triangular flaps inside—the crease will be there already.

12 Complete. Turn the paper over.

13 Gently open the layers from the center to form a bowl.

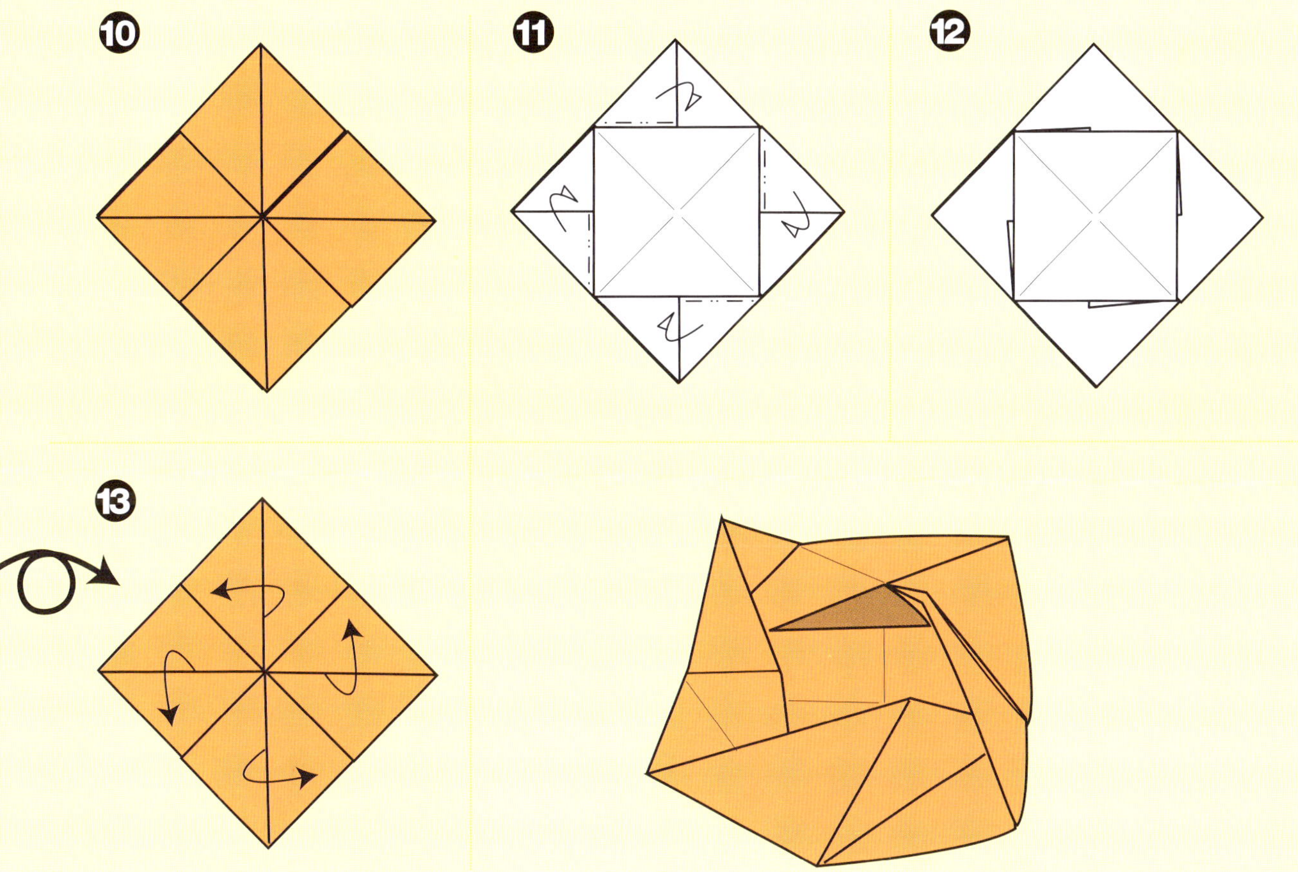

Modular Cube

Modular designs use several origami "units," folded identically, that are designed to have flaps and pockets so they tuck into each other to form geometric shapes. This design is presented to illustrate how you can fold creatively to develop many variations and extensions from an initial idea. With all modular designs, it is important to fold neatly, so that the units fit together snugly. Start with a square, colored side upwards. You'll need six sheets to complete the cube; using two sheets in three different colors makes an attractive result. This design was discovered by Tomoko Fuse and rediscovered by the author!

1. Fold side to opposite side, but only make small pinch marks at either end, to mark the half-way points.
2. Fold in half from side to side.
3. Fold each side to the center. Turn the paper over.
4. Take the folded edges to the center, allowing the layers underneath to flip out.
5. Fold both short edges to meet the pinch marks at the center.
6. Crease firmly, then open the flaps out half way. Make five more identical units.
7. Line up the units as shown, then slide the left one into the pocket of the right one.
8. Add a third unit on the top, interlocking the flaps and pockets as shown.
9. Add the other three, placing the same colour on opposite sides of the cube.

There are many variations to be discovered—try folding in the corners at step 5, for instance.

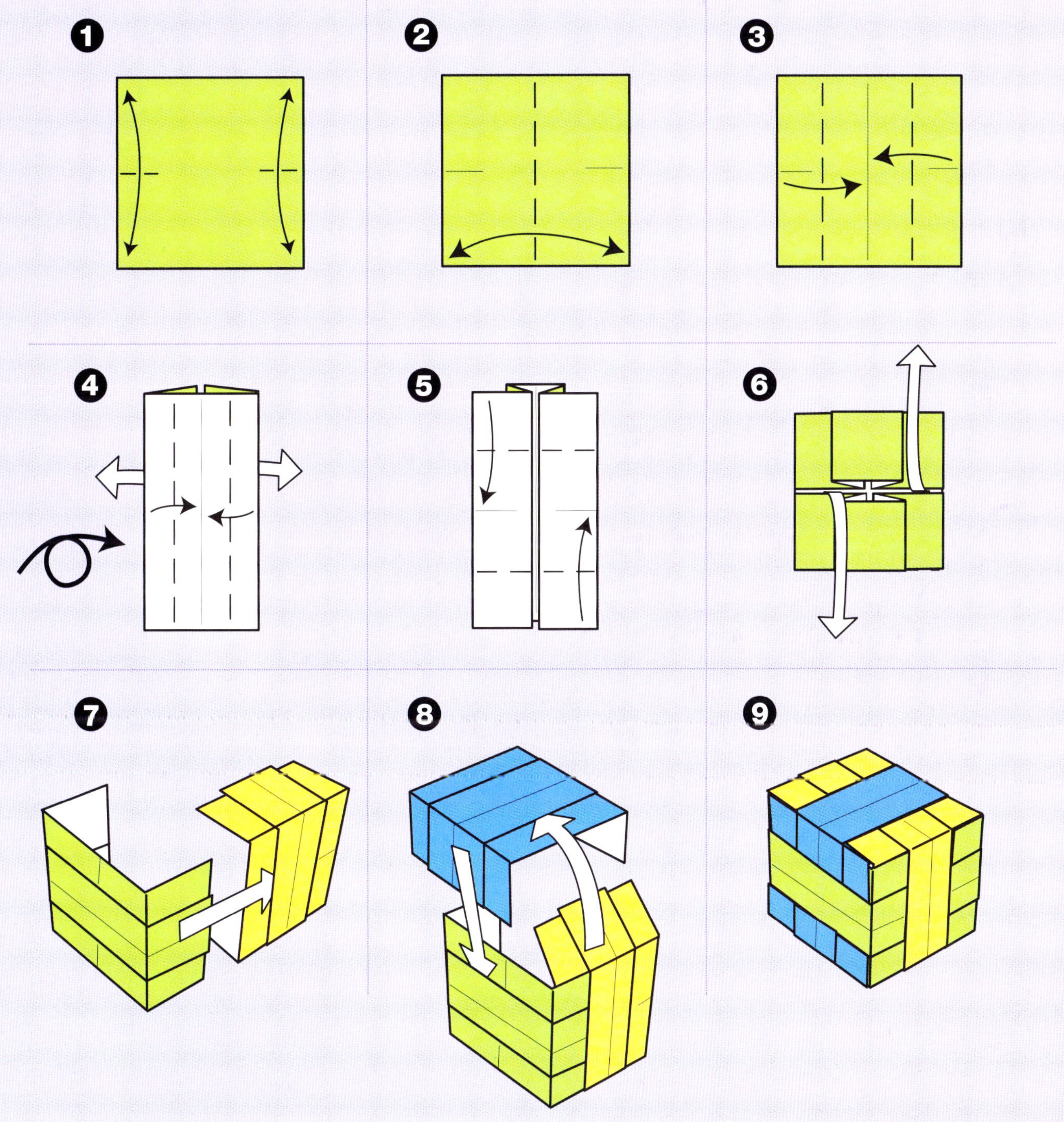
1
2
3
4
5
6
7
8
9

What next?

Once you've folded most (or, hopefully, all) of the designs in this book, you may well have become a convert to the wonderful world of origami. To follow up on your interest, there are a number of places where you can find more designs. Your local library should have a few origami books available. Another good source is the internet, where you can find thousands of diagrams to try out. If you really like a model, why not email the creator and tell them so?

If you are serious about origami, why not join one of the many Origami Societies around the world? You could even join several, just to get their magazines every month. Many societies hold annual conventions, at which paper-folders spend a weekend folding paper and sampling the local delights. The Web will give you lots of information on all aspects of origami, and a Google search will list hundreds of sites.

Credits

Contributors to this book include Kuni Kasahara, Marc Kirschenbaum, Evi Binzinger, John Smith, Siero Takegawa, Francis Ow, Tomoko Fuse, Jason Neale, Andrea Crain, and Marc Kirschenbaum. Also thanks to Mark Robinson (proof-reader extraordinaire).

Biography

Nick Robinson has been folding paper since the early 1980s and has been a member of the British Origami Society for 20 years. He has served on the council for over 10 years. He currently edits the Society's bimonthly magazine and maintains its web site.

Nick spent 4 years as a professional origami teacher, traveling to schools, libraries, youth clubs, hospitals, and art galleries, teaching origami and paper artwork. He has run sessions with people of all ages and physical abilities. Students included the visually- and hearing-impaired.

He has appeared frequently on television in England and Germany, and has fulfilled numerous commissions for magazines, television, and internet advertising campaigns. Over 100 of his original origami creations have been published in 13 countries around the world, including a Japanese newspaper. He has submitted work to many prestigious international exhibitions. In 1994, he was a winner in three of the five categories of the International Alice in Wonderland Origami competition.

Nick has written and illustrated over a dozen origami books, with total worldwide sales approaching half a million.